Scottish Commerci

something different

this symbol in the vehicle lists indicates there is a photo of that vehicle in the book

Many small coachbuilders moved into the bus market in 1946 to satisfy the huge pent-up demand for new buses and coaches. Most went out of business or gave up bus and coach work in or around 1950, when the demand was satisfied and the major bus and coachbuilding firms, having surplus capacity, began to seek orders aggressively. By that time, too, operators were finding that the products of some of the smaller firms left something to be desired. The advent of the underfloor-engined coach came with the authorisation of 30ft-long single-deckers and producing a body for these was often too much for a small, jobbing coachbuilder.

At first glance, Scottish Commercial seems no different from any of these small firms. Its predecessor had a long history of van and lorry bodywork. Mainly an Austin agent, it was operated as a sole trader by its owner and not a limited company. Its 1940s foray into full-size buses was tiny - 16 double-deck bodies and 6 (maybe 8) coach bodies which, like those of many other small coachbuilders, looked a bit strange and ungainly. It may have built some small bus bodies on Austin chassis during the war, but the more this is investigated, the less likely it seems. So why is there anything especially interesting about Scottish Commercial?

Scottish Commercial steel-framed bodied GDF 58 was photographed outside Cardiff General Station.

THE BUS ARCHIVE

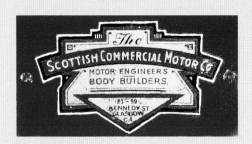

First is that in 1945 it obtained the sole distributorship for Crossley chassis in Scotland. Second, 15 of those double-deck bodies were of three very different designs: a highbridge composite (timber reinforced with steel frame), a lowbridge (also composite) and, extremely unusual for any small coachbuilder, a steel-framed highbridge. Designing the latter was beyond most small and many larger ones - Burlingham's first steel-framed double decker was built in 1951, Massey's in 1952.

Some firms took out a licence or bought in frames from a larger maker - Brockhouse, just down the road from Scottish Commercial, did this with Park Royal in 1946 and in a couple of years would become involved in the Scottish Commercial story. Scottish Commercial, however, seems to have done it more or less on its own, and probably encouraged by Crossley Motors, but maybe without much thought given to the finance and skilled staff it would need if the venture was to be a success.

Third is why, at a time when major operators were desperately short of buses, the government allocated to this tiny firm four of the first 150 Crossley post-war double-deck chassis. No other small firm or operator got any. How did tiny Scottish Commercial get a government allocation of steel for the six steel-framed bodies? And why did it get Crossley's first three post-war single deck chassis?

Then there were the customers for these six. None was originally intended for a Scottish operator. Three were intended for a small Bristol firm, Almondsbury Engineers Ltd's Streamways bus and coach operation located in Penarth, just south of Cardiff, for contract work. After six months or so, Streamways lost that contract and sold the buses to Cardiff Corporation. Two more were for Neath & Cardiff Luxury Coaches' express service; they were delivered, but before they were even licensed, permission to use them on the service was refused by the Traffic Commissioner and they were returned to Scottish Commercial, which then sold them to a Scottish operator. The original client for the sixth is not known, but may have been Almondsbury. Built along with the third Streamways bus, it remained unsold for a few months before going to a small Yorkshire operator.

In November 1947, Thomas Gray bought a major share of Scottish Commercial. He had been director and general manager of Millburn Motors and before that with SMT's dealership. Scottish Commercial's focus appears to have changed from building bodies to being a dealer. Bodies for Crossleys came from Brockhouse, Roe, Santus and Alexander, some of which had slightly misleading maker's transfers that implied they were Scottish Commercial bodies.

A 1949 advert at the time of the Scottish Show, offered at the firm's premises *"a complete new range of Crossley double-deck buses and single-deck coaches by leading builders, available for trial and inspection, plus new and equal to new Austin, Bedford, Commer, Seddon and Vulcan passenger vehicles on view for immediate delivery"*. The dream, insofar as Crossleys were concerned, ended with AEC deciding to cease making Crossley chassis, whereupon Scottish Commercial was downgraded to a simple AEC dealer. It continued supplying vehicles: Karrier refuse collectors to Glasgow and 12 Leyland PD2s to Edinburgh (and even there the story involves a third party which may or may not have been associated with Scottish Commercial's owners), but then slipped into a slow decline, ceasing to trade in 1956.

That is what makes Scottish Commercial a bit different from the average post-war small coachbuilder.

"This whole thing arose from one simple query about the body plate on Cardiff's Scottish Commercial and Alexander bodied Crossley DD42s."

evolution

What became the Scottish Commercial Company started around 1890 as Grant, Cameron & Curle of 83 Kennedy Street, St Rollox, Glasgow - cart-wrights, van and lorry builders. It was not a limited company. Curle left the partnership soon after and Grant left in 1892, leaving Kenneth Cameron as sole owner.

The firm soon occupied 83-99 Kennedy Street. In the 1920s it called itself the Spring, Van and Lorry Factory and built lorry bodies plus a very small number of bus bodies - eight on Thornycroft, Albion and Leyland chassis are known. By 1940 the business sub-name was **The St Rollox Motor Body and Lorry Factory**, with an Austin commercial vehicle agency. Which probably nicely describes its operations.

Cameron died in 1941 and the business was taken over by Francis O'Neill and Thomas Fagan Junior, who renamed it the Scottish Commercial Motor Company – again not a limited company. It seems likely that one or both were on the staff.

In April 1944, O'Neill and Fagan took over the Glasgow-based haulage business of Morgan & Brown and a new limited company, Morgan Brown & Co Ltd, was formed, with Brown, O'Neill and Fagan as directors. It seems that Fagan moved to work full time in this, leaving O'Neill as the sole proprietor of Scottish Commercial. He seems to have had ambitious plans.

In 1945 he managed to obtain the sole distributorship of Crossleys in Scotland. That was something of a coup, for at the time Crossley's military vehicles had a fine reputation, especially with the Royal Air Force during the war. The prototype post-war Crossley chassis looked very good and the firm was about to secure the then largest-ever export order for 1,175 bus chassis to re-equip the war-ravaged Netherlands; in addition, Crossley was planning to introduce a range of medium and heavy lorry chassis. If you were in Scotland and wanted a Crossley, then you had to get it from Scottish Commercial. Unusually for a Scottish firm at the time, and probably with support from Crossley, it sold vehicles into Yorkshire and further afield.

In 1945 Crossley was the first of the bus chassis makers to be authorised to begin post-war production. Of the 150 DD42 chassis that the government authorised Crossley to build in 1945/46, all were allocated by the government – 146 to municipal operators or export, but the other four went to Scottish Commercial, and they were some of the first of the sanction. There was much the same pattern in the next two DD42 sanctions and it was the same for the single-deck SD42 when production started in 1948: the first home market SD42 chassis went to Scottish Commercial.

In 1946 J R Harrison joined the firm as Technical Manager. He appears to have had in-depth experience at Crossley before the war and to have brought with him knowledge of Crossley's in-house steel-framed design, which had been developed before the war but not got into production, and of Ayrshire Metals, Crossley's supplier of the cold-rolled sections used for the framing. Harrison was the bodywork expert in an IRTE Brains Trust in January 1947.

January 10, 1947.

SCOTTISH I.R.T.E. BRAINS TRUST

AT a meeting of the Scottish Centre of the Institute of Road Transport Engineers, on January 13, at 7.30 p.m., at the Institution of Engineers and Shipbuilders, 39, Elmbank Street, Glasgow, a "Brains Trust" will be held. The subjects and members are:— Brakes: H. S. G. Browning, A.I.R.T.E., A.M.I.M.I., area manager, Brake Linings, Ltd.; Chassis and Petrol Engines: C. E. F. Blaber, A.M.I.A.E., Albion Motors, Ltd.; Oil: J. Gillespie, M.I.E.S., area general manager, W. B. Dick and Co., Ltd.; Bodywork: J. R. Harrison, technical manager, the Scottish Commercial Motor Co.; Tyres: H. Mountford, technical department, India Tyre and Rubber Co., Ltd.; Diesel Engines: F. Gilchrist, depot superintendent, the Associated Equipment Co., Ltd.

Below is a view of Kennedy Street in Glasgow, near Scottish Commercial's premises.

THE SCOTTISH COMMERCIAL MOTOR CO.

NOTICE is hereby given that the undersigned Francis O'Neill, of 14 Cleveden Drive, Burnside, Rutherglen, and Thomas Fagan, junior, of 71 Whifflet Street, Coatbridge, have commenced trading as THE SCOTTISH COMMERCIAL MOTOR CO., at 83 99 Kennedy Street, Glasgow, as from the first day of September 1941.

F. O'NEILL.
T. FAGAN.

Signed by the above named Francis O'Neill and Thomas Fagan, junior, at Glasgow, on the 18th day of September 1941, in presence of

ALEXANDER WATERSON, 69 Cadder Road, Glasgow, Salesman.
HELEN M. C. LEE, 92 Greenlees Road, Cambuslang, Cashier.

THE Firm of the SCOTTISH COMMERCIAL MOTOR COMPANY, carrying on business as Motor Engineers at ninety nine Kennedy Street, Glasgow, has been DISSOLVED as on the twenty-first day of March nineteen hundred and forty four, by mutual consent, by the retiral therefrom of the Subscriber Thomas Fagan, one of the Partners.

The Business will continue to be carried on by the Subscriber Francis O'Neill on his own account and under the name of the SCOTTISH COMMERCIAL MOTOR COMPANY. Francis O'Neill is authorised to uplift all the debts due to, and he will discharge the whole debts and liabilities of, the Firm.

Dated at Glasgow, the twenty first day of March nineteen hundred and forty-four.

THOMAS FAGAN.
Witnesses to the Signature of the said Thomas Fagan
HELEN M. C. LEE, Cashier, 99 Kennedy Street, Glasgow.
HUGH GALLACHER, Solicitor, British Linen Bank Chambers, Coatbridge.

FRANCIS O'NEILL.
Witnesses to the Signature of the said Francis O'Neill —
HELEN M. C. LEE, Cashier, 99 Kennedy Street, Glasgow.
HUGH GALLACHER, Solicitor, British Linen Bank Chambers, Coatbridge.

Source: Edinburgh Gazette
April 27 1944.
Morgan Brown and Co, Ltd
Private company. Registered in Edinburgh 27/4/44.
Cap. £1,200 in 41 shares.
To acquire the business of a haulage contractor, carried on at 52, Carmichael Street, Glasgow. and to adopt an agreement between David R. Brown and H. Gallacher (see below).
Directors:—
David R. Brown, 462, Paisley Road W., Glasgow; Francis O'Neill; 14, Cleveden Drive, Burnside, Rutherglen; Thomas Fagan, 71, Whifflet Street, Glasgow.
Reg. office: 52, Carmichael Street, Glasgow.

Hugh Gallacher was a lawyer acting for Fagan and O'Neill.

Company struck off the register 1/3/49 for providing no returns for 2 years.

Kennedy Street was in an industrial area and during 1947 a lease was taken on a workshop/building in Dobbies Loan near the centre of Glasgow.

In November 1947, a new partner bought into the bus firm. The Commercial Motor reported, *"Thomas Gray, formerly associated with the Scottish Motor Traction Co., Ltd., and until recently director and general manager of Millburn Motors Ltd., has acquired an interest in the Scottish Commercial Motor Co., Glasgow. The company is an Austin commercial-vehicle dealer and bodybuilder."*

Gray appears to have initiated a move away from bodybuilding (bodies in work or committed to being completed) and towards a dealership, ordering chassis and bodies from makers for stock and selling them, much in the style of Millburn Motors. There is no further reference to Harrison at Scottish Commercial.

With the ending of production of Crossley chassis, as a dealer the firm seems have gone into a steady decline, closing in 1956.

On this page is a nearside view of ASN 62, which ran with Barrass of Doncaster, who traded as Don Motors, from November 1950 to November 1955.

On the opposite page is an offside view of the same bus, having lost the Motors section of its fleetname.

**THE BUS ARCHIVE
ROGER HOLMES**

ASN 53 chassis number 93317
composite frame H30/26R
new in Dec 1946 to H Brown & Son (Red Bus Service) of Garelochhead

ASN 62 chassis number 93316
composite frame H30/26R
new in Dec 1946 to H Brown & Son (Red Bus Service) of Garelochhead

4

1946
the highbridge composite double deckers

The first Crossley DD42 chassis sanction was for 150 (93201-93350), all on government allocation with priority going to big operators. Of the 150, seven went for export, 139 went to municipal operators such as Manchester, Salford and Bolton, so it was curious that tiny Scottish Commercial got the other four (93312/14/16/17), which were delivered in the spring of 1946.

Scottish Commercial bodied them and even here the story is strange, for two were composite framed and the other two, of a very different design, were steel framed.

The two composite ones were sold to Brown, Garelochhead and went into service in December 1946 as ASN 53 and ASN 62. The body had flared lower-deck side panels and Manchester-style dipped front windows. In 1950, the ownership of Brown's business changed, by which time ASN 62 passed to a Yorkshire operator (J H Barrass ("Don"), Doncaster) - an odd Scotland/England connection that will recur in the Scottish Commercial tale.

1946-1947
the steel-framed highbridge double deckers

Remarkably, in parallel with the two lowbridge bodies, work also began on the first two steel-framed (all-metal) bodies of strikingly different design. They also had Manchester-style dipped windows at the front and a careful study of the body's dimensions shows it was based on Crossley Motors' all-steel frame, but without the suspended platform and raised rear windows of Crossley's body. The framing was probably sourced as a kit from Crossley's metal sections supplier, Ayrshire Metals Ltd, a Clydeside shipbuilder that had moved from shipbuilding into the manufacture of cold rolled steel sections in the 1930s. This suggests that Scottish Commercial had more than simple access to Crossley's designs, probably through J R Harrison. Design-wise the result looked ill at ease.

Eight bodies, two designs (one composite, one steel-framed) was a very ambitious thing for a small firm to do. Nevertheless, it did it and the two steel-framed buses were delivered at the same time as the composite ones. Why do both? Because Crossley didn't design/produce a lowbridge version of its steel-frame until early 1947.

In 1946, new buses were allocated by the government, often without any local knowledge and ignoring operators' requirements. This seems to have happened when the two steel-framed bodied Crossleys were allotted to Neath & Cardiff Luxury Coaches Ltd (N&C), who ran single-deck coaches on a busy and tightly timed express service between Cardiff and Swansea. Short of vehicles, it asked for some double-deckers and was allocated two Crossleys, but (and maybe fortunately) before N&C could discover the shortcomings of the Crossley engine on such work, what seems to have been a government error put an end to the plan.

The bridge under Neath Station needed lowbridge double-deckers. This was well known to all the local operators, but seemingly not to those in London allocating new buses; Western Welsh and South Wales, hardly friends of N&C, would not be minded to raise the issue. The two Crossleys were highbridge and when delivered were far too tall to go under the bridge. After a trial run confirmed this, they appear to have been directed back to Scottish Commercial and swiftly advertised for sale. The advert used a strange hand-drawn sketch of a pre-war Manchester Corporation Crossley Mancunian Streamliner in a version of the livery that was applied to only a handful of the very first Streamliners back in 1936. It was not one that Crossley had used to sell its products, but can only have been produced by someone familiar with pre-war Crossleys, probably Harrison.

In mid-1947, the two buses were sold to Ayrshire Bus Owners (A1 Service) of Ardrossan, becoming BCS 889/90, and Neath & Cardiff got some single deckers.

The rear end of GDF 58 in the view on this page is very similar to the Crossley body.

Not so the front end, where the body was fitted to the standard dash panel, which Crossley removed on its own bodies. Cover up the cab and the Crossley similarity is clear.

ALAN B CROSS

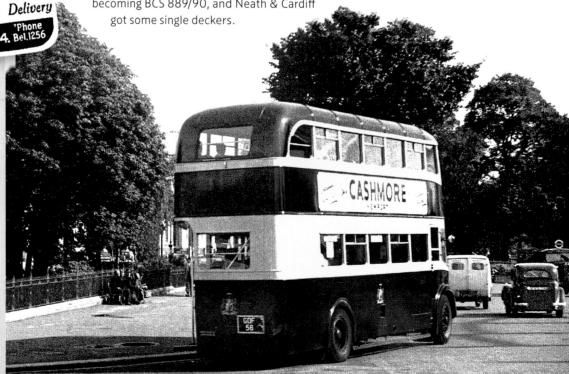

They had a tall look about them (and they were, at 14ft 8½in), recognisably the same as a 1946 Crossley body, similarly tall.

Below, Cardiff 24 was by the bus station in the city with Wood Street in the background.

GEOFFREY MORANT

Compare them with this picture of Manchester 2945 on the right.

MUSEUM OF TRANSPORT, GREATER MANCHESTER

BCS 889 chassis number 93312

steel frame H30/26R

ordered in 1946 by Neath & Cardiff of Neath in Glamorgan

returned to Scottish Commercial in Jun 1947 and
sold to Ayrshire Bus Owners (A1 Service) of Ardrossan

BCS 890 chassis number 93314

steel frame H30/26R

ordered in 1946 by Neath & Cardiff of Neath in Glamorgan

returned to Scottish Commercial in May 1947 and
sold to Ayrshire Bus Owners (A1 Service) of Ardrossan

📷 **GDF 58** chassis number 93825

steel frame H30/26R

new in Mar 1947 to Almondsbury Engineers (Streamways)
of Almondsbury, Bristol

sold to Cardiff in Dec 1947

📷 **GDG 456** chassis number 93876

steel frame H30/26R

new in Jun 1947 to Almondsbury Engineers Ltd (Streamways)
of Almondsbury, Bristol

sold to Cardiff in Dec 1947

📷 **FDT 202** chassis number 94068

steel frame H30/26R

new in Mar 1948 to George Ennifer (Blue Ensign) of Doncaster

📷 **EBO 103** chassis number 94074

steel frame H30/26R

new in Jul 1948 to Cardiff (as its 25)

this bus was ordered by Almondsbury Engineers in Aug 1947 and allocated
registration HAD 141

the works contract ended while the bus was in build and
the order was taken over by Cardiff

Meanwhile, two more DD42 chassis (chassis numbers 93825/76) had arrived late in 1946 and work had started on all-steel bodies for them. They had already been sold to an equally surprising customer, once again a long way from Scotland.

Almondsbury Engineers Ltd of Almondsbury, Bristol, had a Cardiff-based coach operation (Streamways, Penarth) that had gained a works contract that needed double-deckers quickly. Speculation is that the contract was for government work such as defence. It ordered three from Scottish Commercial, probably through Crossley's own sales staff. The first two were delivered in March and June of 1947 (GDF 58, GDG 456), as soon as Scottish Commercial finished them. They ran for Streamways until the end of 1947, when the contract suddenly ended. Again probably with help from Crossley sales staff, they were then sold to Cardiff Corporation, which was very short of buses. Cardiff also took over the contract for the third, for which the chassis had not yet been delivered, ordering a further six Scottish Commercial-bodied DD42s at the same time – these are covered further on.

A fifth steel-framed body went onto chassis 94068, which arrived in mid-1947. Whether it was originally intended for Almondsbury or N&C is not known, but it was a year before it was completed and sold to a Yorkshire operator, George Ennifer (Blue Line) of Doncaster, who ran FDT 202 successfully until into the 1960s; by contrast, he quickly got rid of his Scottish Commercial-bodied SD42 coach.

The sixth and final one (on 94074) was to have been the third for Almondsbury; it was allocated a Gloucestershire registration (HAD 141), but the order was taken over by Cardiff Corporation and, after some delay while contracts were rearranged, it was delivered to them as EBO 103 in July 1948. The three buses looked tall and they were. At 14ft 8½ inches high they were restricted to a few services, mainly the 23 to Whitchurch, the 26 to Snowden Road, Ely and the 38 to Rhiwbina Deri. They were withdrawn in 1961 – about right for a 1946 Crossley frame.

1947-1948
three lowbridge composite double deckers

Designing an in-house lowbridge steel frame would have been too big a task and therefore, with no Crossley lowbridge frame kits available at the time, the next bodies were composite. More or less a lowbridge version of the bodies on ASN 53 and ASN 62, they may have already been in work for a delayed A1 Crossley DD42 order. Over the period May 1947 to July 1948 they were fitted to Foden chassis, one going to A1 and the other two to Carruthers, Dumfries. Interestingly, all three featured the 1936 Manchester-style streamline marking on the upper deck.

The lowbridge bodies weren't particularly durable. For example, CAG 76's body was scrapped in 1955 and replaced with an ex-Liverpool pre-war Weymann body.

SW 7255 chassis number 25782

composite L27/26R

new in Aug 1947 to Carruthers of New Abbey

CAG 76 chassis number 25798

composite L27/26R

new in Jan 1948 to Ayrshire Bus Owners (A1 Service) of Ardrossan

---

SW 7540 chassis number 27324

composite L27/26R

new in Jul 1948 to Carruthers of New Abbey

Carruthers' impressive-looking SW 7255 was in Dumfries on 9 June 1958 in the picture here, turning out of Whitesands into Buccleuch Street.

The Royal Burgh of Dumfries on the River Nith, the largest town in South West Scotland, is often referred to as The Queen of the South. It was local poet David Dunbar, who in 1857 stood for Parliament in the General Election and, in one of his addresses, first described Dumfries as Queen of the South. The name is also used for the town's football team.

Dumfries has been an important market town since Roman times and was once home to Scotland's national bard, Robert Burns.

Dumfries was also the scene of Robert the Bruce's murder of his great rival the Red Comyn at Grey Friar's Kirk in 1306, which started off a bloody civil war.

J S COCKSHOTT ARCHIVE

OS 6922 chassis number 97301

Scottish Commercial/Binnie (see text) C35F
new in Sep 1948 to McKeand of Newton Stewart

ASN 348 chassis number 97302

Scottish Commercial C33F
new in Nov 1947 to Clydebank Co-op Society

FGE 768 chassis number 97303

Scottish Commercial C33F
new in Jan 1948 to Miller of Calderbank

ASN 587 chassis number 97313

Scottish Commercial C33F
new in Jul 1948 to Clydebank Co-op Society

ASN 588 chassis number 97320

Scottish Commercial C33F
new in Jul 1948 to Clydebank Co-op Society

DVD 928 chassis number 97327

Scottish Commercial/Binnie? (see text) C35F
new in Oct 1948 to Baxter of Airdrie as its 40

FDT 804 chassis number 97365

Scottish Commercial C33F
new in Sep 1948 to Ennifer (Blue Ensign) of Doncaster

FUS 608 chassis number 293J3 (Dennis Lancet III)

Scottish Commercial C33F
new in Jul 1948 to De Duca of Glasgow

1947-1948
coach bodies

I n parallel with the highbridge composite, highbridge steel-frame and lowbridge composite bodies, Scottish Commercial also started building composite-framed coach bodies.

Crossley began production of home market single-deck chassis in 1947 with a sanction for 75 chassis and, remarkably, in April 1947 Scottish Commercial got the first three. The coach body was as strange looking as the double deckers. Six coaches were built, five on SD42s and one (FUS 608) on a Dennis Lancet chassis. All were delivered in 1947/1948 – the first in December 1947 and the last, the Dennis, in October 1948.

Something odd happened to chassis 97301, and to 97327. Both are supposed to have been bodied by Binnie of Wishaw, one going to McKeand of Newton Stewart and the other to Baxter of Airdrie. Strangely, they were not licenced until September/October 1948, a gap of 12-18 months from chassis delivery. It is surely odd for Crossley's very first home-market SD42 chassis to lie around for a year or more at a time when coaches were in short supply. No picture of either has been found and it seems likely that Scottish Commercial started to body them, along with the other four, but perhaps with a lack of skilled staff and the arrival of Thomas Gray, work stopped and the part completed coaches passed to Binnie to finish.

One of the coaches seems to have remained unsold for four or five months after its completion and, along with the last of the all-metal bodied DD42s, George Ennifer of Doncaster bought it. Crossley's Yorkshire area salesman of the time appears to have sold it – he was noted for being pushy. One operator casually mentioned needing a new coach to this salesman, who turned up the following week with a brand new Burlingham-bodied SD42 and, *"you said you needed one, so here it is, I have registered it in your name and arranged for the deposit to be paid"*. The operator had an SD42 and didn't much want another, but gave in.

FDT 804 shown below didn't last long with Ennifer, who sold it in January 1952.

In the picture below, in worn condition, it was with General of Chester-le-Street in June 1958.

When the Foy family acquired De Duca's business, FUS 608, shown opposite, was transferred to their other acquisition, until then Brown of Garelochhead. The firm was reconstituted as Garelochhead Coach Services. The coaches carried names of Lochs.

J S COCKSHOTT ARCHIVE

On this page are Crossley's publicity shots of brand new Glasgow C1 above (EGA 75) and Duncan's, DVA 670 on the right.

CROSSLEY MOTORS ARCHIVE

Delivered in 1948/49, Glasgow's Crossley bodied AEC Regents were numbered A21-A70 (FYS 121-170). Opposite was A28 in service in July 1958.

J S COCKSHOTT ARCHIVE

1947
orders from Glasgow

Two complete Crossley-bodied DD42s also arrived with Scottish Commercial in 1947. The first, for Glasgow, had Brockhouse turbo-transmitter transmission. Delivered in April, along with the first coach chassis, it had started life as Crossley's second post-war prototype chassis, 92902. The chassis was then updated to DD42 specification and added on to the end of the 938 sanction of 100 chassis, with the odd chassis number 93900A, (93901 upwards were already in build). It was registered EGA 75.

A second complete Crossley DD42 with a constant-mesh gearbox, was delivered in September 1947. It was finished in Manchester's pre-war Streamline livery, which Manchester had given up in 1945, and was thoroughly out of date in 1946. It was sold at once to Duncan of Law and was later passed to Hugh Love of Lesmahagow.

Glasgow was unimpressed with the DD42 chassis but not the body and ordered 50 bodies on new AEC Regent III chassis. The bodies were to Glasgow's specification and, being a large batch, the order had to be placed directly with Crossley, which delivered all 50 in 1948/49.

📷 **EGA 75** chassis number 93900A

Crossley H30/26R

new in Apr 1947 to Glasgow Corporation as its C1

📷 **DVA 670** chassis number 94051

Crossley H30/26R

new in Oct 1947 to Duncan of Law in Lanarkshire

1948-1949
a change in emphasis

Nine more DD42 chassis were delivered in March 1948. Two were intended for the (by then delayed) A1 lowbridge order. All were to have had Scottish Commercial lowbridge bodies.

With no client for three of them, three were sent to Santus, which fitted them with coach bodies – there was a ready market for coaches, even on double-deck chassis, and Crossley's sales staff seem to have had customers waiting locally in the Manchester area. One, bought by Woodcock of Heskin, got a Bellhouse Hartwell body, its intended Santus body being put onto a refurbished Leyland Titan TD2 chassis. The coach-bodied DD42s were unique and it was a strange thing to do, involving changes to the chassis springs (otherwise the ride would be very hard) and also to the body pillars.

The delays in building bodies, probably due to shortage of skilled staff, must have caused Scottish Commercial cashflow difficulties, it being a sole trader firm. Notably, haulage firm Morgan Brown Ltd ceased trading about this time. The other six chassis were sent to Roe for lowbridge bodies. Delivered in June and July, they were sold to Baxter (three), A1 (one), Smith (SCWS) (one) and Wemyss Bros (one).

Whether two South Shields highbridge Roe-bodied DD42s with adjacent Roe numbers (GO 2766/67) were anything to do with Scottish Commercial is a matter of speculation – their chassis numbers (94155/122) are close to the three Santus coaches and the six Roe double-deckers.

KMB 106 chassis number 94111
Santus C33F
new in May 1948 to Altrincham Coachways

JTE 523 chassis number 94125
Santus C33F
new in Jul 1948 to Cash of Urmston, Lancashire

ordered as lowbridge double deck for Ayrshire Bus Owners A1, order deferred and chassis bodied as coach in Sep 1948 for Woodcock of Heskin (may not have run for Cash)

JTF 840 chassis number 94143
Bellhouse Hartwell C33F
new in Sep 1948 to Woodcock of Heskin, Lancs

ordered as lowbridge double deck for Ayrshire Bus Owners, order deferred and chassis intended to be bodied as coach by Santus

Woodcock instead put the Santus body on a second-hand TD2 chassis that became JTF 716, fitting the DD42 with the Bellhouse Hartwell body ordered for the TD2

GGA 75 chassis number 94108
Roe GO2760 L27/26R
new in Jul 1948 to Smith of Barrhead
(Scottish Cooperative Wholesale Society)

EVA 104 chassis number 94140
Roe GO2762 L27/26R
new in Sep 1948 to Baxter of Aidrie 28

EVA 105 chassis number 94141
Roe GO2763 L27/26R
new in Aug 1948 to Baxter of Aidrie 29

EVA 179 chassis number 94136
Roe GO2761 L27/26R
new in Sep 1948 to Baxter of Aidrie 33

CAG 928 chassis number 94142
Roe GO2764 L27/26R
new in Oct 1948 to Ayrshire Bus Owners A1

CST 671 chassis number 94160
Roe GO2765 L27/26R
new in Sep 1948 to Wemyss Bros of Ardersier

On some of the bought-in bodies (Cardiff's Alexander ones, for example), the maker's body plate was turned front to back and the Scottish Commercial transfer applied to the reverse (by then facing) side - something which understandably misled observers.
On the right is the plate on Alexander-bodied Cardiff 46.

DAVID BEILBY

The last to be withdrawn, 46 has been preserved and in the picture below looks most resplendent in its maroon and ivory livery.

THE BUS ARCHIVE / ROY MARSHALL

Desperately short of buses, Cardiff had ordered six more lowbridge-bodied Scottish Commercial metal-framed DD42s. Having no steel-framed lowbridge body itself and Roe's being composite, Scottish Commercial negotiated with Cardiff to allow it to sub-contract the bodies to Alexander, which involved a few months' waiting time.

The chassis arrived towards the end of 1948, Alexander fitted them with its then current Leyland-derived body, and they went into service in June 1949. Retrofitted with downdraught engines, they ran until 1963-1966, the now preserved 46 being the last to go.

For several years the only lowbridge buses in the Cardiff fleet were these Alexander bodied Crossleys, their primary duty being Cardiff's share of the 36 to Tredegar, until the AEC Bridgemasters arrived in 1960.

In the picture below Cardiff 44 was in Blackwood, working from Tredegar back to Cardiff.

THE BUS ARCHIVE / ROY MARSHALL

EBO 899   chassis number 94751
Alexander 3649 L27/26R   new in Jun 1949 to Cardiff as 45

EBO 896   chassis number 94752
Alexander 3647 L27/26R   new in Jun 1949 to Cardiff as 42

EBO 897   chassis number 94753
Alexander 3646 L27/26R   new in Jun 1949 to Cardiff as 43

📷 **EBO 898**   chassis number 94757
Alexander 3648 L27/26R   new in Jun 1949 to Cardiff as 44

📷 **EBO 900**   chassis number 94855
Alexander 3650 L27/26R   new in Jun 1949 to Cardiff as 46

EBO 901   chassis number 94859
Alexander 3651 L27/26R   new in Jun 1949 to Cardiff as 51

On these pages are pictures of two of the A1 buses, CCS 800 and DAG 123.

The bodies were not good and both buses were scrapped in 1958/59. The angled flitch plates on the lower-deck windows of CCS 800 are probably evidence of some in-service strengthening.

THE BUS ARCHIVE

The last Scottish Commercial bodies were four more lowbridge composite ones, three of which went to the A1 partnership and one to Baxter, plus a highbridge one on Crossley frames for Glasgow, covered on a later page. The work seems to have been done slowly – one in March 1949, the Baxter in May, and the two final A1 vehicles in December 1949, with the last, built on downdraught-engined DD42 chassis 94938, supplied to Scottish Commercial as a demonstrator chassis. They were composite, but the design differed in detail from those on the Fodens.

The first, CCS 800 for A1, differed in several details from the Baxter and the two last A1s. The bodies weren't durable – all were scrapped in or around 1958/59, with, as recounted further on, that on EVD 406 being condemned in 1954.

📷 **CCS 800** chassis number 94756

composite L27/28R

new in Mar 1949 to Ayrshire Bus Owners A1

📷 **EVD 406** chassis number 94758

composite L27/26R

new in Jun 1949 to Baxter of Aidrie as 34

sold in Sep 1954 to Wood of Mirfield and
rebodied by Roe as H31/25R in Apr 1955

📷 **DAG 123** chassis number 94929

composite L27/26R

new in Jan 1950 to Ayrshire Bus Owners A1

📷 **DCS 340** chassis number 94938

composite L27/26R

new in Jan 1950 to Ayrshire Bus Owners A1

this bus had been supplied in late 1949 to
Scottish Commercial for use as downdraught
demonstrator chassis

what was A1 Service?

To counter the growing big operator, Scottish General Transport, many of the smaller bus operators in the area bound by Largs to the north, Kilmarnock to the east and Ayr to the south, grouped together in 1925 to form the Ayrshire Bus Owners Association. Following the 1930 Road Traffic Act, this more formally became the Ayrshire Bus Owners (A1 Service) Ltd in 1931, with a base in Ardrossan, although each member continued to own and maintain its own vehicles.

A livery of blue and cream with a maroon belt was introduced and over the following years A1 remained a successful co-operative. When any members left, usually through retirement or ill-health, their vehicles and shares in the company were sold on to other members. This continued well into the late 1990s.

By the mid-1990s, the double-decked trunk Ardrossan/Kilmarnock service was the only bit that was in any way profitable – conductors were still being employed on this route, and mechanical problems were becoming increasingly frequent in its ageing fleet. Some members wanted out and offered their shares for sale.

An agreement was reached with Western Scottish, which had just recently become a Stagecoach subsidiary, and the company was sold for £4.3 million in January 1995.

The story of the EVD 406 is told on this page, and on the opposite page is this bus with its new Roe body at Wood's Longcauseway terminus in Dewsbury. It ran in service until 1968.

THE BUS ARCHIVE ROBIN HANNAY

There is an unfortunate twist to the story of EVD 406. In 1953 Baxter sold it to a dealer, probably North's of Leeds, which in turn sold it later that year to Joseph Wood of Mirfield, who had five Crossley SD42 coaches and needed a new double-decker for his Dewsbury to Mirfield stage service. On the face of it, a four year-old DD42 was a good purchase.

The pictures on this page show the bus with the dealer above and, nicely repainted in Wood's black and cream livery, at the Mirfield terminus of Wood's Dewsbury to Mirfield route on 23 September 1954.

It was not in service in the picture and there is some doubt that it ever ran in service for Wood's thus, as shortly after this the Yorkshire Traffic Area Vehicle Examiner condemned the body framing as beyond repair and it was sent to Roe for a new highbridge body. The bus then ran for Wood until 1968 and was kept on withdrawal. In the late 1990s it was restored to splendid condition by his son, Colin, and is now in the Dewsbury Bus Museum.

top picture THE BUS ARCHIVE
left picture J S COCKSHOTT ARCHIVE

Austins

The Austin commercial dealership continued through all these changes and van and lorry bodies continued to be built on Austin chassis.

There is a report that, in 1948, Scottish Commercial built a 16-seat bus body on an Austin chassis for Skye operator, Elgol Bus Service. This was JS 7986, and is shown in the picture below. The body may not actually have been built by Scottish Commercial; it is more likely to have been sourced from another builder.

RICHARD GADSBY COLLECTION

1948-1949
Brockhouse

Thomas Gray then appears to have developed a relationship with Brockhouse. It seems that with Scottish Commercial giving up building bus bodies, J R Harrison had departed.

The West Bromwich-based Brockhouse group had several interests in the bus industry. It had acquired the Sunbeam Trolleybus Company from Rootes and later sold it to Guy Motors. Its Southport works made Crossley's turbo transmitter. The Clydeside branch had an agreement with Park Royal to use its steel frames in double-deckers and had its own design of composite-framed single-deckers.

In April 1948, Scottish Commercial took into stock seven SD42 chassis intended to be fitted with bus bodies. Whether Scottish Commercial ever planned to body them itself is questionable – it had no single-deck bus design. The bodies were ordered from Brockhouse.

Unable to do the work, Brockhouse in turn ordered them from Roe. The order was then reduced to four; Brockhouse bought these four chassis from Scottish Commercial and it took delivery at the end of October 1948. Two were licensed (but not taxed) in Brockhouse's name at Dumbarton motor tax office (ASN 813/14), and then all four were sold by Brockhouse to Edinburgh Corporation, which was very short of buses, entering service there a month later with Edinburgh registration numbers GSF 334-337. The bodies were recorded by Roe as 'semi-coach', with 32 seats and saloon luggage racks. They were altered to 34 seats before entering service at Edinburgh, but retained their luggage racks.

It has long been claimed the four were intended for Waldie of Helensburgh, allegedly having been registered ASN 814-817. This is proven wrong from both Roe's delivery records and Crossley's chassis records. Waldie had a fleet of six and one elderly 29-seat bus. The story appears to have been a mistake in a publication of 50 years ago, and much copied since. The other three chassis were bodied by Brockhouse as coaches and went to Smith of Barrhead (SCWS).

Above is GSF 335 with Edinburgh Corporation.

GAVIN BOOTH

The parcel racks are just visible in the picture below right of GSF 334 when it was owned by Jackson of Auchinleith after sale by Edinburgh.

**THE BUS ARCHIVE
ROY MARSHALL**

The picture at the top of the opposite page shows GGE 937 after it was sold on by Smith's to Garner of Bridge of Weir in June 1958.

J S COCKSHOTT ARCHIVE

The other picture opposite shows GGE 935 when new. Note the folding door.

CROSSLEY ARCHIVE

GSF 334 chassis number 97601
Roe GO2776 B34F

B32F semi-coach body. registered ASN 814 but not taxed or sold. Altered to 34 seats and sold to Edinburgh, A1, in Dec 1948.

GSF 335 chassis number 97605
Roe GO2777 B34F

B32F semi-coach body, not sold. Altered to 34 seats and sold to Edinburgh, A2, in Dec 1948.

GSF 336 chassis number 97620
Roe GO2775 B34F

B32F semi-coach body, registered ASN 813 but not taxed or sold. Altered to 34 seats and sold to Edinburgh, A3, in Dec 1948.

GSF 337 chassis number 97635
Roe GO2778 B34F

B32F semi-coach body, not sold. Altered to 34 seats and sold to Edinburgh, A4, in Dec 1948.

These 3 were new May 1949 to Smith of Barrhead

GGE 935 chassis number 97730
Brockhouse FC33F

GGE 936 chassis number 97845
Brockhouse FC33F

GGE 937 chassis number 97889
Brockhouse FC33F

1948-1950
dealing in coaches

A further 25 Crossley SD42 coaches were supplied through Scottish Commercial as a dealer, with 11 of those getting coach bodies by Santus. All but one went to Scottish operators, the exception being the one that went to Ennifer of Doncaster (again). Available on short delivery, Santus bodies were not the most durable; Leith of Sanquhar later chopped off the body behind the cab of theirs and replaced it with most of an ex-Alexander body.

The other 14 were bodied by Brockhouse and sold to Scottish operators, notably 10 coaches to Aberdeen Corporation, though quite who contracted for what between Scottish Commercial (chassis) and Brockhouse (bodies) is unclear.

EVA 503   chassis number 97693
Santus C33F   new in Dec 1948 to Stephen of Biggar

GSP 282   chassis number 97694
Santus C33F   new in Jan 1949 to Robertson of Freuchie

GDT 116   chassis number 97768
Santus C33F   new in Jan 1949 to Ennifer of Doncaster (Blue Ensign)

ESA 900   chassis number 97786
Santus C33F   new in Jan 1949 to McIntyre of Bucksburn

CCS 887   chassis number 97894
Santus C33F   new in Mar 1949 to Ayrshire Bus Owners (A1 Service)

CCS 802   chassis number 97923
Santus C33F   new in Feb 1949 to Law of Prestwick

EVD 216   chassis number 98009
Santus C33F   new in Apr 1949 to Jackson of Auchenheath

CCS 875   chassis number 98052
Santus C33F   new in Sep 1949 to Law of Prestwick

EVD 455   chassis number 98084
Santus C33F   new in Jun 1949 to McFadyean of Baillieston

📷 **KSM 40**   chassis number 98085
Santus C33F   new in Jul 1949 to Leith of Sanquhar

rebodied by Leith with Alexander bus body from Leyland WG 7508 marrying this to the cab/front bulkhead of the Santus body about 1962

JP 7964   chassis number 98092
Santus C33F   new in Oct 1949 to Duncan of Law

The two photographs here show Leith of Sanquhar's KSM 40.

On this page is a view taken in August 1960 of the vehicle with its Santus body.

The shot on the opposite page was taken in January 1964 after most of its Santus body had been removed and replaced by a secondhand Alexander body.

J S COCKSHOTT ARCHIVE

GGG 703
Brockhouse FC33F
chassis number 97979
new in May 1949 to SCWS in Glasgow

GGG 704
Brockhouse FC33F
chassis number 97998
new in July 1949 to SCWS in Glasgow
(Blane of Kilmarnock)

DRG 686
Brockhouse FC29F
chassis number 98004
new in May 1950 to Aberdeen - 86

DRG 687
Brockhouse FC29F
chassis number 98005
new in May 1950 to Aberdeen - 87

DRG 688
Brockhouse FC29F
chassis number 98068
new in May 1950 to Aberdeen - 88

DRG 689
Brockhouse FC29F
chassis number 98072
new in May 1950 to Aberdeen - 89

DRG 690
Brockhouse FC29F
chassis number 98076
new in May 1950 to Aberdeen - 90

DRG 691
Brockhouse FC29F
chassis number 98079
new in May 1950 to Aberdeen - 91

DRG 692
Brockhouse FC29F
chassis number 98089
new in May 1950 to Aberdeen - 92

DRG 693
Brockhouse FC29F
chassis number 98090
new in May 1950 to Aberdeen - 93

DRG 694
Brockhouse FC29F
chassis number 98095
new in May 1950 to Aberdeen - 94

DRG 695
Brockhouse FC29F
chassis number 98096
new in May 1950 to Aberdeen - 95

CWG 188
Brockhouse FC33F
chassis number 98102
new in Jan 1950 to Fitzcharles of Grangemouth

NKR 529
Brockhouse FC33F
chassis number 98123
new in Sep 1949 to Scottish Commercial
as stock demonstrator; bought by Molins
Machine Co Ltd of Saunderton in Bucks and
later passed into preservation

With Scottish Commercial's Crossley distributorship ending, other dealers began to supply Crossley coaches into Scotland, for example the Windover-bodied ones listed below.

The November 1949 advert on the right captures the firm's changed emphasis, and maybe the fact it could not afford a stand at the show. Crossleys on display would have been downdraught DD42 chassis (94938), a complete lowbridge DD42 (DAG 123), and Brockhouse-bodied SD42s (CWG 188 and what became NKR 529), retrofitted with a downdraught engine. Nothing is known for the Austin, Bedford, Commer, Seddon and Vulcan.

| **GGE 939** | chassis number 97813 |
| Windover C33F | new in Apr 1949 to SCWS of Glasgow |

| **GGE 938** | chassis number 97840 |
| Windover C33F | new in Apr 1949 to SCWS of Glasgow |

| **GGE 940** | chassis number 97880 |
| Windover C33F | new in Apr 1949 to SCWS of Glasgow |

| **GGG 723** | chassis number 97939 |
| Windover C33F | new in May 1949 to SCWS of Glasgow |

| **GGG 725** | chassis number 98061 |
| Windover C33F | new in May 1949 to SCWS of Glasgow |

Below left is a photo of Glasgow's Crossley-bodied AR293. Crossley used the parts ordered by Scottish Commercial and the result looked more like a Scottish Commercial body than a Crossley.

JOHN KAYE

1950-1951
more Glasgows

In 1949/50 Glasgow Corporation decided to rebody 45 1937/38 AEC Regents. The general manager's plan was that they would be bodied by Scottish Aviation, as explained in the Scottish Aviation section of this book.

However, the Transport Committee wanted the work placed locally and so Scottish Commercial gained an order for ten, which were to have Crossley frames of the same design as the 50 new Regent IIIs supplied two years previously.

It is perhaps a sign of staff or cash problems that the firm finished only one. AR291 (BUS 184) was completed slowly and delivered in December 1950.

Long before that, however, Scottish Commercial arranged to subcontract the others to Crossley. Scottish Commercial passed the parts, such as windows pans and window ventilators to Crossley, which used them instead of its standard items and delivered AR 286-290, 292-295 (BUS 176/77/79/83/82/71/85/66/72) in January to March 1951.

1950-1952
the run down

With AEC now firmly in charge at Crossley, and although the downdraught version had solved many of the Crossley engine's shortcomings, the ACV board decided to end manufacture of the SD42 and DD42 chassis. In 1950 Scottish Commercial found itself downgraded from being the Crossley distributor for Scotland to being simply one of many agents for AEC vehicles, its Crossley-based business at an end. Up against the big dealer firms such as SMT, Stanley Hughes, Lancashire Motor Traders, Kirkby and the like, Scottish Commercial had little chance.

It continued as a dealer, supplying, for example, nine Karrier refuse collectors to Glasgow in 1951 (which was the firm's last mention in Commercial Motor). In 1952, Scottish Commercial supplied some stock Leyland-bodied Titan PD2s to Edinburgh, a complex story involving another haulier, George Rodger (Motherwell) Ltd, which made a vain attempt to enter the bus supply market.

Rodger ran a fleet of Leyland Comet trucks and in addition to the PD2s had also ordered 12 Leyland Royal Tiger coaches, which it eventually sold through Millburn to Hutchison (2) and Alexander (10).

Scottish Commercial closed down in mid-1956. It may be coincidence or a reflection of trading difficulties in general that George Rodger (Motherwell) Ltd and its (by then) parent, London Scottish Transport Ltd, were made bankrupt at the same time.

In the picture above, JWS 69 was still in primer and with its as-built indicators.

GAVIN BOOTH COLLECTION

Gavin Booth records . . .

These buses have always been intriguing, as Edinburgh Corporation Transport minutes show that the first 11 were never formally authorised, but the remaining 10 were, on 11 November 1952. The first 11 were delivered in January and July 1952, carrying current registration marks in the JSF and JWS series; normally Edinburgh would order registrations well in advance of new deliveries.

The remaining 10, again carrying current registrations in the KFS series, were authorised in November as being "immediately available". Delivery started that same month and had been completed by the end of 1952. Leyland photos exist showing a grey-painted PD2/12 carrying an Edinburgh registration, but with non-standard destination blind boxes. The buses were rebuilt with Edinburgh standard blind displays and were painted at Shrubhill Works in Edinburgh.

Leyland records show that the first seven of the buses had been ordered by George Rodger (Motherwell) Ltd, a Scottish haulier, presumably with an eye to break into the bus market. Rodger never did, and these seven buses are the ones that carry JSF registrations. Chassis numbers for the 21 PD2/12s cover a span from 514xxx to 521xxx, and the unladen weight of the buses varied widely. Most were 56-seaters, but five of the later buses, nos.251-5, were 58-seaters, with extra inward-facing bench seats above the rear axle in the lower saloon.

in retrospect

t is hard to see how or why Scottish Commercial's optimistic course - building highbridge and lowbridge double deckers and coaches and selling several in England - could have happened without direct involvement and support from Crossley. Crossley had lost its pre-war heavy vehicle Scottish agent. With virtually all Crossley output going to the military or Manchester Corporation, the agent had had nothing to sell and Crossley needed a new one.

After the war, however, Crossley planned to build medium and heavy lorries in addition to buses and, with its own bus body building capacity taken up with the Netherlands order, could well have seen Scottish Commercial as a useful backup for Crossley's English clients.

The sale to AEC changed how Crossley was run and that almost certainly would have affected Scottish Commercial even before AEC stopped making Crossley chassis. In retrospect, what Scottish Commercial did was brave but, sadly, it became the hapless victim of a corporate merger.

wartime – the small Austin buses
by Richard Gadsby

As Austin agents for Scotland, Scottish Commercial was able to supply about 27 Austin goods chassis to bus operators between 1943 and 1945 for essential PSV work in the remoter parts of the Scottish highlands and islands, where the requirement was for robust vehicles in challenging terrains and for vehicles capable also of carrying mail and goods. Almost half of the vehicles were supplied to operators on the island of Lewis, at a time when some seven hundred RAF personnel were involved in the operation of anti-submarine planes from Stornoway aerodrome. Lewis Castle in Stornoway was also used as a naval hospital and for accommodation, thereby significantly increasing the requirement for bus facilities.

This provision for Scottish operators by The Ministry of Supply appears to be unique - the only single decker normally available was of course the Bedford OWB with standard utility bodywork. The bus bodies have been claimed to be by Scottish Commercial, but this does not seem to be the case. It is likely that all the bus bodies for these Austins were built by smaller Scottish coachbuilders at a time when the major bodybuilders were fully committed elsewhere with the war effort.

From photographic evidence and contemporary vehicle recording by the likes of Jimmy Blair and Jimmy Lacroix, we know that at least four of the bodies were built by Cadogan of Perth, at least another four by Croft of Glasgow, and at least two by Walker of Aberdeen. It is also known that these three coachbuilders, along with Dickson of Dundee, were selected in 1943 by the authorities to *provide repair work, with a monthly capacity of four single-deckers*. It is likely, therefore, that the building of the bodies for the Austin vehicles was part of this agreement and, although Scottish Commercial supplied them, none were actually bodied by it.

Two of the vehicles we now believe to have had Cadogan bodies (JS 6703/08) were actually recorded by Messrs Blair and Lacroix as having Scottish Commercial bodies. This was later confirmed by Robert Grieves to Richard Gadsby in the late 1980s.

Cadogan-bodied NS 1898 on the opposite page belonged to MacLennan of Diabaig in Sutherland. It was new in 1943 to Lochinver-Invershin Motor Co, passing to Sutherland Transport & Trading Co Ltd of Lairg in 1948, and then to MacLennan by December 1955.

RICHARD GADSBY COLLECTION

Walker-bodied BST 79 (above) was supplied new in 1943 to Beaton of Portree. It was photographed at the Kyleakin Pier in September 1952 awaiting ferry passengers from the mainland, long before the building of Skye Bridge.

ALAN CROSS

JS 6708 on the left was with Galson-Stornoway Motor Services on Lewis, new in 1943. It shows very strong characteristics of a Cadogan body - compare with NS 1898 on the opposite page.

THE BUS ARCHIVE / ROY MARSHALL

Based on personal observation of JS 6708
(at least), Robert mentioned that the bodies had
Scottish Commercial transfers. It is now known,
however, that Scottish Commercial also fixed
similar plates to other bodies supplied by them as
a dealer but which they had not built – this was
a not uncommon practice by some dealers.

After further research, it was concluded that
the two vehicles were almost certainly bodied
by Cadogan, given the close similarity of design
to two other known Cadogan bodies supplied
on Austin chassis at this time. The Croft and
the Walker bodies were very different, and it is
unlikely that Scottish Commercial would have
built bodies to Cadogan design at this time.
All in all, there is no evidence that Scottish
Commercial built any bus bodies during the
Second World War.

SCOTTISH AVIATION
PRESTWICK   AYRSHIRE LTD

Scottish Aviation
something innovative

S cottish Aviation was almost the opposite of Scottish Commercial in every way. A look at the company and its products perhaps highlights not only how over-ambitious Scottish Commercial was, but also that, even if a company had exceptional resources, good modern technology, an excellent reputation for quality and a workforce of 2,400, it was very difficult to break into the bus and coach building market, even at a time of very high demand.

Both companies exited the bus and coachbuilding business, as did many other aspiring firms, large and small – for example, Beccols, Bellhouse Hartwell, Brockhouse, Churchill, Dutfield, Gurney Nutting, Longford, Metalcraft, Santus, Trans United, Whitson, Windover, to name only a few. It was hard to compete with the might of Duple, Burlingham and Plaxton for coaches; for bus bodies, it was even harder against firms like Metro Cammell, Park Royal, Roe, Crossley and Alexander.

background & development

Scottish College of Aviation Ltd was formed in August 1935 as a flying training school for Royal Air Force officers. The first directors were the Marquis of Douglas & Clydesdale (later 14th Duke of Hamilton) and David McIntyre (the owner of Prestwick airfield), who were actually the first pilots to fly over Mount Everest. A contract with the Air Ministry was signed in October 1935 and training activity started four months later at Prestwick. De Havilland provided the aircraft and one third of the capital and 20 Tiger Moths were used. The company was re-named Scottish Aviation Ltd in March 1936.

The training activity continued until March 1941, when the arrival of the United States Air Force, with large numbers of personnel and aircraft, caused Scottish Aviation to take up aircraft fitting, maintenance and conversion. It quickly gained a very high reputation for its work for both the British and American Air Forces, becoming the sole European contractor for some of the latter's fleet of aircraft.

The splendid art deco Palace of Engineering, built for the Empire Exhibition in Glasgow, was reassembled at Prestwick in 1940 to provide extra capacity to the existing hangars. Separately, an air ferry service from Prestwick Airport across the North Atlantic was established. Peacetime flights started in January 1946 from Prestwick to Belfast, and these lasted until November 1960.

buses & coaches

The end of the war saw a considerable drop in aircraft work and Scottish Aviation looked for new markets for its skills. One was the development of a light alloy bus/coach body, using the company's in-house aircraft design experience with the material. This included designing body frames using stress calculation methods normally applied in aircraft, but new to bus and coach design, and the stressed skin construction used in aircraft engineering, the bodies being double-skinned on the sides and roof.

While aluminium alloy, when used in this way, was as strong as its steel and timber counterparts, there was a large reduction in weight – half a ton on a double-decker – and the result was some of the first lightweight bodies that were also very robust and durable. In December 1947, a considerable part of the factory space was re-equipped for the construction of bus and coach bodies. The firm had high hopes, for bodies were not the only new product; the company also made cabs for agricultural tractors, and the like.

A Light Alloy Cab
FOR THE FORDSON MAJOR TRACTOR

This cab is built entirely of light alloys and weighs only 110 lbs. It is, however, strong and rugged enough to stand up to the hardest wear. It can be fitted or removed from the tractor within a minute, and is light enough to be handled by one man.

PRESTWICK, AYRSHIRE

Scottish Aviation built 133 bodies, compared with Scottish Commercial's 22. The table on the right summarises production; it is complete so far as we know and uses the dates the bodies were built; some entered service a year or more later.

A popular Scottish Aviation product was lightweight bolt-on cabs for Fordson and Ferguson agricultural tractors.

Production ran into the hundreds, from 1946 into the 1960s. The adverts here are from 1959.

ALLAN CONDIE COLLECTION

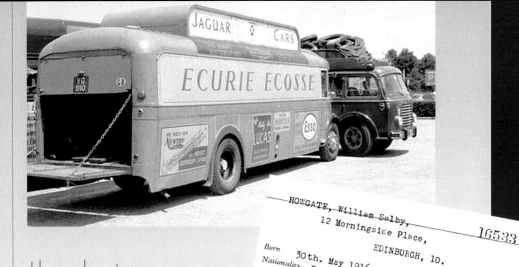

HOWGATE, William Selby,
12 Morningside Place,
EDINBURGH, 10.   16533
Born   30th. May 1916   at   Leeds, Yorkshire.
Nationality British
Rank, Regiment, Profession   Ground Engineer.
Certificate taken on   Moth - Gipsy 1 - 90 h.p.
At Bedford School of Flying.
Date 14.11.38

the designer
(William) Selby Howgate

B orn in Leeds in 1916 and educated at Oxford's Magdalen School, Selby Howgate became an aircraft ground engineer. He gained his pilot's licence in 1938 and became an aeronautical designer, later joining Scottish Aviation. Being interested in styling and also involved in motor sport, he designed the single and double-deck Scottish Aviation bodies.

Recruited by Alexander's coachbuilding operation as Chief Engineer in 1948, he influenced the style of Scottish Aviation's bodies on Commers.

He was responsible for Alexander's move to alloy frames in 1953 but was unhappy about having to move to steel framing in the late 1950s to satisfy BET orders, despite efforts to persuade the BET's Chief Engineer, Š Č Vince, to adopt alloy.

His involvement in motor sport (along with Managing Director Ronnie Alexander) was with Bill Murray's Ecurie Ecosse Jaguar racing team, for which Howgate designed, and Alexander built, the famous car transporter, VSG 7. The chassis was a Commer TS3.

Selby Howgate became Alexander's Engineering Director in 1967; sadly, this was cut short by his untimely death due to a motoring accident in 1969. Alexander returned to alloy framing in 1972.

1948 - 12 bodies

single deck

2	AEC Regal III
2	Commer Q4
1	Crossley SD42/7
3	Foden PVSC
1	Leyland Tiger TS6 rebody
2	Leyland Tiger PS1

double-deck

1	Foden PVD6

1949 - 57 bodies

single deck

11	Albion Victor FT39N
12	Commer Q4
32	Commer Commando
2	TSM K6MA7

1950/1 - 64 bodies

single deck

2	AEC Regal III
3	Albion Valkyrie CX9
13	Albion Victor FT39N
1	Albion Victor FT3AB
2	Albion KP71NW
19	Commer Q4
1	Ford ET6
1	Leyland Tiger PS2
2	Maudslay Marathon III

double-deck

10	AEC Regent rebody
5	Albion Venturer
5	Daimler CVD6

total 133

Based on a Commer TS3 chassis, this famous vehicle on the left, VGS 7, was designed by Selby Howgate and built (at considerable cost) by Alexander, whose managing director was involved with Ecurie Ecosse. Its rather less well-known predecessor was WG 1110 - an Alexander-bodied Leyland TS4, previously Alexander P121. It became the Ecurie Ecosse transporter in 1954.

MICHAEL EYRE COLLECTION

the full size heavy chassis coaches

Among the companies that expressed an interest in Scottish Aviation bus bodies were SMT, Glasgow Corporation and Albion Motors. 44 Foden chassis were to be fitted with Scottish Aviation bodies, but this was reduced to three single-deckers and one double-decker, apparently due to the government's allocation restrictions on material for chassis production.

Nevertheless, the company claimed that 74 firm orders for bodies had been received by the start of bodybuilding, although government restrictions subsequently affected this. In Spring 1948, Scottish Aviation was planning production of two bus bodies per week, with an increase to five planned.

A prototype was built and later used as a demonstrator. This was followed by a batch of 10, delivered during 1948, some of which were fully fronted. The first coach body delivered was on an AEC Regal III chassis for Northern Roadways of Glasgow in March 1948.

These two black and white views of, above, the nearside of Dunoon Motor Services SB 7369 and the rear of Warren (Altonian) of Hants GOU 586, above right, show the awkwardly shaped back end. It was strange, as the rest of the design was coherent, if continental.

SCOTTISH AVIATION / THE BUS ARCHIVE

Prototype CCS 61, below, was sold to A1 Service (Hunter), which ran it until late 1965. It then went to Bannatyne of Blackwaterfoot on Arran, who ran it until 1971 - a remarkable life of 23 years. Few 1948 coaches achieved that.

GEOFFREY MORANT

The half-cab body had a full canopy, not uncommon in Scotland, but used by few other British post-war coach designs. Scottish Aviation stated the design was based on continental practice – almost all continental and American coach design had straight waist rails, as did some Alexander bodies, but the British fashion, dating from pre-war streamlining, was for curved ones. Bus and coach operators tended to be very conservative and this would limit the appeal of Scottish Aviation's straight-waisted designs.

The full-front version, built on four chassis (shown in the table) looked more modern, and sympathetic paintwork treatment helped, but the rear end corner had some awkward angles: neither bus nor coach. The coach interior was nicely fitted out and well finished, but to some of the coach hiring public (and some operators), the external appearance had a pre-war bus flavour and this probably affected sales. At 1 ton 15 cwt the body was some 5-7cwt lighter than a steel-framed or composite coach body, which weighed around 2 tons; a chassis was typically just over 4 tons. Thus, when a full-load passenger weight of about 2 tons was added, the total saving was only about 5-7cwt in 8 tons (160cwt).

The next batch had a tidier rear end and a neater, more gently curved front canopy that gave them less of a bus look. Parts may have been built for 10 but with the dwindling demand for new coaches, only eight were built before the company gave up the bus and coach industry. A 1949 order from Alexander for bodies for 22 Albion Valkyrie CX9s was cancelled, probably because of a mixture of over-ordering and the apparent withdrawal of Albion from making passenger chassis.

The dates in the table are the dates the vehicle entered service.

Bus-looking or not, the bodies proved very durable. Most ran until 1966 – a very creditable life of 16-18 years, much longer than many from larger, better-known coachbuilders.

	LAYOUT	REG NO.	CHASSIS	CHASSIS NO.	DELIVERED	DELIVERED TO
📷	FC32F	CCS 61	Foden PVSC6	27268	**Aug 1948**	Scottish Aviation demonstrator
	C32F	FGG 171	AEC Regal III	0962102	**Mar 1948**	Northern Roadways of Glasgow
	C32F	FGG 173	AEC Regal III	0962104	**May 1948**	Northern Roadways of Glasgow
📷	FC33F	SB 7369	Foden PVSC6	26676	**May 1948**	Dunoon Motor Services
📷	FC32F	DVD 782	Foden PVSC5	27260	**Jun 1948**	Tennant of Forth
	FC32F	DFR 346	Leyland Tiger PS1/1	481548	**Sep 1948**	Blackhurst of Blackpool
	C33F	DFR 362	Leyland Tiger PS1/1	481202	**Sep 1948**	Blackhurst of Blackpool
	C32F	GGB 362	Crossley SD42/7	97372	**Oct 1948**	Northern Roadways of Glasgow
	C32F	FV 4626	Leyland Tiger TS6	4414	**Nov 1948**	Swarbrick of Cleveleys
📷	C33F	GOU 586	TSM K6MA7	9287	**Jan 1949**	Warren of Alton
📷	C33F	GOU 732	TSM K6MA7	9276	**Mar 1949**	Warren of Alton
📷	C35F	DAG 607	AEC Regal III	9621A1112	**Feb 1950**	A1 Service of Ardrossan
📷	FC35F	KSM 566	Albion CX9	58079K	**Mar 1950**	Gibson of Moffat
	B35F	FVA 812	Albion CX9	58076L	**Mar 1950**	Carmichael of Glenboig
	C33F	KOM 102	AEC Regal III	9621E1136	**Mar 1950**	Newton of Birmingham
	B39F	KUP 928	Albion CX9	58076H	**Mar 1950**	Milburn Motors
📷	C33F	XS 6983	Maudslay Marathon III	70594	**Mar 1950**	Young of Paisley 200
	C33F	XS 6984	Maudslay Marathon III	70596	**Mar 1950**	Young of Paisley 201
📷	C35F	SB 8160	Leyland Tiger PS2/3	496203	**Jul 1950**	McConnachie of Campbeltown

angular rear

improved rounded style with flush glazing

Warren had two Scottish Aviation bodied coaches, both on Tilling Stevens chassis. Originally with Meadows engines, he changed them to Gardners. GOU 732 had a remarkable life. In service until 1974, it was then withdrawn, but reinstated in 1976 and ran until autumn 1980, when it was bought for preservation.

In the picture above it was taking part in the London to Brighton rally, here just by Palace Pier turning into Grand Junction Road to head along Brighton's sea front.

JOHN WALKER

Gibson of Moffat in Dumfriesshire had two Scottish Aviation bodied Albion coaches with similar registration numbers. KSM 566 was a Valkyrie, and KSM 655 a Victor with a similar looking body. Both were fitted out as coaches and are correctly described as such, although their straight-line waist made them look somewhat bus-like.

KSM 566 ran until 1963 and was then scrapped. The picture on the right was taken in Dumfries Bus Station in Whitesands alongside the River Nith on 9 June 1958.

The spire poking up behind the coach is in Laurieknowe and belongs to the Victorian church built for the Maxwelltown Free Church in 1865-66 to a design by local architect, James Barbour.

J S COCKSHOTT ARCHIVE

The second batch of heavy-chassis coaches had a neater rear end more in tune with the market.

The side view above of newly completed Albion Valkyrie KUP 928 shows the maker's posters and signs featuring the alloy body and its weight of only 35 cwt. It was supplied to dealer Millburn, whose name it carried here as legal owner.

The rear view is of Maudslay Marathon XS 6984. New to Young's Bus Service of Paisley, this passed, along with the business, to Western SMT, in which fleet it was numbered 2201.

SCOTTISH AVIATION / JOHN SINCLAIR

Armstrong of Ebchester in County Durham bought the Albion Valkyrie in the picture above, KUP 928, from Millburn. It was equipped with 39 bus seats and here was working a stage service to Burnhope. The bus was withdrawn in 1960.

R C DAVIS

Parked alongside Yeates bodied Leyland Tiger PS1 GFU 623 at Brodick Pier on the Isle of Arran on the right, AEC Regal III DAG 607 looked somewhat bus-like, although it was every bit as nicely fitted out and, in the longer term, more durable.

Both were owned by Lennox of Whiting Bay, although by then the Lennox company had changed its name to Arran Transport & Trading Co Ltd.

ALISTAIR DOUGLAS

The final Scottish Aviation body on a heavy chassis was SB 8160, which was bought by A & P McConnachie Ltd of Campbeltown, where this picture of it above was taken. The combination of lightweight body and 9.8-litre O.600 engine would have resulted in (potentially at least) an exciting trip. McConnachie ran it for 16 years.

THE BUS ARCHIVE
ROY MARSHALL

On the left is the rear of DAG 607 mentioned on the left-hand page. Note the horizontal brightwork trim behind the rear wheel and compare this with the angled version on the Tiger above.

ALISTAIR DOUGLAS

These two pictures are of what was the more 'normal' design for a coach of the late 1940s and demonstrate how far Scottish Aviation's 'continental' styling was from what most operators expected.

The picture above is perhaps more interesting in that it is by another aircraft firm trying to break into coach work, Bellhouse Hartwell. Like those of Scottish Aviation, Bellhouse Hartwell's bodies were very well built and finished but they were of the type of styling that customers better understood.

This was Manchester-based H Hackett's JNE 382, new in 1948. Bellhouse Hartwell built around 150 bodies, all coaches.

BELLHOUSE HARTWELL ARCHIVE

flowing lines & dipping waists of mainstream coachbuilders

These two Leylands show the more usual flowing and dipping lines found on contemporary British coach styling. The coach on the left was a Duple rebodied pre-war Tiger TS7 and next to it a post-war Burlingham bodied Tiger PS1.

New to Ribble, they were with Loch Lomond - Loch Katrine Services Ltd of Inversnaid when photographed in 1964 at Stronachlachar Pier on Loch Katrine in the Trossachs. That's Cruinn Bheinn rising up in the background of this tranquil scene.

GEOFFREY MORANT

the small coaches

An important order came from W Alexander & Sons for 28 coach bodies on Commer Commando chassis, which went into service during mid-1949 (six for subsidiary David Lawson). This combination proved popular with Scottish independents and 65 were eventually built, some on ex-War Department Commer Q4 military surplus chassis, which were similar to the postwar Commando. All were petrol-engined and all except a sole example on a Ford ET6 chassis had sliding roofs.

All but one went to Scottish operators, and the exception went only just over the border, to Hartness of Penrith. Like the larger coaches, they also proved durable and, again, many ran until the mid- to late 1960s, the Alexander ones passing to new owners at various dates from 1953 to 1961. The only variation in the body seems to have been the introduction of rubber-mounted glazing for the side windows in mid-1949, with a first installation on CMS 287 and then CMS 288, 290 and from CMS 292 onwards.

The final small body was built on the then new Ford ET6 chassis, presumably with a view to opening up a new market to rival the ubiquitous Bedford OB. Bellhouse Hartwell, another aspiring coachbuilder coming from an aircraft background, did something similar, again with a straight waist rail. It was all to no avail, as in late 1950 Bedford introduced the forward-control SB. With a Duple body an SB cost £2,190, the same price as an OB but with 33 seats, and it killed the market for normal-control coaches. Commer withdrew the Commando and replaced it with the forward-control Avenger that was an upmarket SB equivalent, as the Commando was to the OB.

Bellhouse Hartwell persevered with coaches a few years longer than Scottish Aviation, but as the aviation market recovered, like Scottish Aviation, it gave up coaches and returned to aircraft work.

Like the firm's other coach bodies, the sole Scottish Aviation ET6 had a remarkable life, running in service on Shetland for 28 years and then passing into preservation in 1978.

This picture, taken in August 1960 at Stark's Dunbar depot, shows SS 7607 (C9), a Commer Q4 with Scottish Aviation body, new in 1950.

It was in the Stark's dark green colours for use on the firm's own services. A proportion of the fleet was disguised as SMT vehicles as part of an arrangement for Stark's vehicles to run SMT's Dunbar-Edinburgh service.

J S COCKSHOTT ARCHIVE

LAYOUT	REG NO.	CHASSIS	CHASSIS NO.	DELIVERED	DELIVERED TO
C31F	GGA 797	Commer Q4	15B9464S	**Sep 1948**	Thomson of West Calder
C31F	GGB 596	Commer Q4	15B9290S	**Dec 1948**	Thomson of West Calder
C31F	CCS 926	Commer Q4	18B1316S	**Mar 1949**	Paterson of Dalry
C31F	EVD 214	Commer Q4	15B9870S	**Apr 1949**	Rae of Wishaw
C35F	GSF16	Commer Commando	17A1111	**Apr 1949**	Rae of Wishaw
C29F	CMS 2	Commer Commando	17A1265	**Apr 1949**	Alexander C1
C29F	CMS 3	Commer Commando	17A1087	**Apr 1949**	Alexander C2
C29F	CMS 4	Commer Commando	17A0739	**Apr 1949**	Alexander C3
C29F	CMS 5	Commer Commando	17A0846	**May 1949**	Alexander C4
C29F	CMS 6	Commer Commando	17A0842	**May 1949**	Alexander C5
C29F	CMS 7	Commer Commando	17A0766	**May 1949**	Alexander C6
C29F	CMS 8	Commer Commando	17A0950	**May 1949**	Alexander C7
C29F	CMS 9	Commer Commando	17A0848	**Jun 1949**	Lawson C8
C29F	CMS 10	Commer Commando	17A0797	**Jun 1949**	Lawson C9
C29F	CMS 11	Commer Commando	17A0812	**Jun 1949**	Lawson C10

	LAYOUT	REG NO.	CHASSIS	CHASSIS NO.	DELIVERED	DELIVERED TO
📷	C29F	CMS 283	Commer Commando	17A0718	Jun 1949	Lawson C11
	C29F	CMS 284	Commer Commando	17A0967	Jun 1949	Lawson C12
	C29F	CMS 285	Commer Commando	17A0973	Jun 1949	Lawson C13
	C29F	CMS 286	Commer Commando	17A0850	Jul 1949	Alexander C14
	C29F	CMS 287	Commer Commando	17A1314	Jun 1949	Alexander C15
	C29F	CMS 288	Commer Commando	17A0997	Jul 1949	Alexander C16
	C29F	CMS 289	Commer Commando	17A0860	Jul 1949	Alexander C17
	C29F	CMS 290	Commer Commando	17A1155	Jul 1949	Alexander C18
📷	C29F	CMS 291	Commer Commando	17A1310	Jun 1949	Alexander C19
📷	C29F	CMS 292	Commer Commando	17A0857	Jul 1949	Alexander C20
	C29F	CMS 293	Commer Commando	17A0974	Jul 1949	Alexander C21
	C29F	CMS 294	Commer Commando	17A0908	Jul 1949	Alexander C22
	C29F	CMS 295	Commer Commando	17A0829	Jul 1949	Alexander C23
	C29F	CMS 296	Commer Commando	17A0713	Jul 1949	Alexander C24
	C29F	CMS 297	Commer Commando	17A1085	Jul 1949	Alexander C25
	C29F	CMS 298	Commer Commando	17A0909	Jul 1949	Alexander C26
	C29F	CMS 299	Commer Commando	17A0851	Jul 1949	Alexander C27
📷	C29F	CMS 300	Commer Commando	17A0984	Jul 1949	Alexander C28
	C29F	CMS 598	Commer Q4	18B2266S	Jun 1949	Gielty, Bridge of Allan
	C30F	GGG 830	Commer Commando	17A1298	May 1949	Taylor of Glasgow
📷	C29F	CSD 178	Commer Q4	18B0545S	May 1949	Bingham of Girvan
	C29F	SB 7717	Commer Commando	17A1304	Jun 1949	Highland Hotel of Glendaruel
	C31F	EVD 529	Commer Q4	15B8477S	Jun 1949	Rae of Wishaw
	C31F	EVD 531	Commer Q4	18B1622S	Jun 1949	Murray of Larkhall
📷	C29F	GUS 129	Commer Q4	18B1529S	Jun 1949	Taylor of Glasgow
	C33F	JSM 953	Commer Commando	17A1260	Jun 1949	Elliot of Lockerbie
	C29F	SJ 1261	Commer Q4	15B9045S	Jul 1949	Newton of Brodick
	C29F	GWS 710	Commer Q4	15B6469S	Jul 1949	Downes of Colinton
	DP29F	JAO 748	Commer Q4	15B2276S	Jul 1949	Hartness of Penrith
	C29F	HFG 591	Commer Q4	15B9067S	Sep 1949	Robertson of Freuchie
	C29F	DAG 303	Commer Q4	15A2591S	Sep 1949	Kennedy of Maybole
	C33F	DAG 907	Commer Q4	18B1518S	Apr 1950	Kennedy of Maybole
📷	C29F	GSR 244	Commer Q4	18B1670S	Apr 1950	Meffan of Kirriemuir
	C29F	GSR 269	Commer Q4	18B0472S	Apr 1950	Fearn of Kirriemuir
	C29F	DES 198	Commer Q4	18B1051S	Apr 1950	Wefare Transport, Aberfoyle
	C29F	FVA 858	Commer Q4	15B8679S	Apr 1950	Marshall of Baillieston
	C29F	HGE 969	Commer Q4	18B1861S	Apr 1950	Patterson Motors of Glasgow
	C33F	CWG 589	Commer Q4	15B0878S	Jun 1950	Gielty of Bridge of Allan
📷	C26F	SJ 1315	Commer Q4	18B0450S	Jun 1950	Morrison of Millport
	C33F	SS 7602	Commer Q4	15B9112S	Jun 1950	Starks of Dunbar C8
📷	C31F	SS 7607	Commer Q4	15B8747S	Jun 1950	Starks of Dunbar C9
	C31F	DCS 118	Commer Q4	18B3719S	Jun 1950	Steele of Stevenston
	C29F	DES 389	Commer Q4	18B2268S	Jun 1950	Brown of Callandar
	C33F	HGG 248	Commer Q4	18B1533S	Jun 1950	Summers of Glasgow
	C33F	XS 7068	Commer Q4	18B0966S	Jun 1950	MacKenzie of Ullapool
	C31F	DCS 105	Commer Q4	15B8087S	Jun 1950	Martin of Newmilns
	C33F	DCS 150	Commer Q4	18B1772S	Jun 1950	Martin of Newmilns
	C33F	SJ 1325	Commer Q4	15A1211S	Jun 1950	Robertson of Blackwaterfoot
	C33F	DCS 153	Commer Q4	15B0736S	Aug 1950	McCall of Kilmarnock
	C32F	BSN 388	Commer Q4	15B5119S	Oct 1950	Frazer of Helensburgh
📷	C29F	PS 2001	Ford ET6	7235576	Oct 1950	Ganson of Lerwick Jan 1951

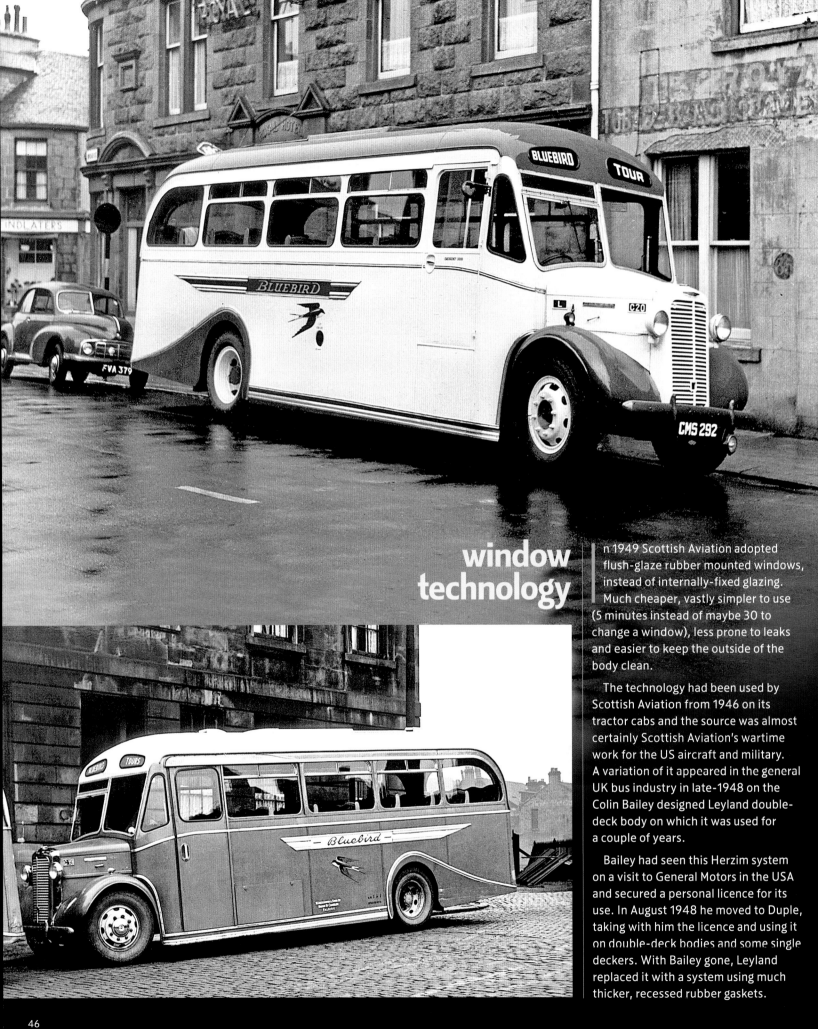

window technology

n 1949 Scottish Aviation adopted flush-glaze rubber mounted windows, instead of internally-fixed glazing. Much cheaper, vastly simpler to use (5 minutes instead of maybe 30 to change a window), less prone to leaks and easier to keep the outside of the body clean.

The technology had been used by Scottish Aviation from 1946 on its tractor cabs and the source was almost certainly Scottish Aviation's wartime work for the US aircraft and military. A variation of it appeared in the general UK bus industry in late-1948 on the Colin Bailey designed Leyland double-deck body on which it was used for a couple of years.

Bailey had seen this Herzim system on a visit to General Motors in the USA and secured a personal licence for its use. In August 1948 he moved to Duple, taking with him the licence and using it on double-deck bodies and some single deckers. With Bailey gone, Leyland replaced it with a system using much thicker, recessed rubber gaskets.

The UK firm Hallam Sleigh and Cheston (Widney) also developed a similar system to the Herzim; it was generally adopted by the bus industry in the 1950s, notably on Metro Cammell's Orion body.

Scottish Aviation's was independent of all this. It was introduced on the Commers in mid-1949 – in the case of the Alexanders, on CMS 287 (CMS 291 was the last of the internal glazed ones).

The second build of bodies for heavy chassis followed suit, as did all the Albion Victor bodies, the Glasgow double-deckers, and the bodies for the two experimental Albion KP71NWs.

The two pictures on the left show Alexander C19 (CMS 291) in the lower view, which was the last built with internal glazing and, in the upper view, in later livery, C20 (CMS 292) was one of the first with flush glazing.

The most noticeable difference is the three side windows below the opening vents.

**ALLAN CONDIE COLLECTION
from ALEXANDER**

Some of the last Leyland bodies with the Herzim system were Manchester's 3265-3299, new in 1950 and shown below left.

MUSEUM OF TRANSPORT, MANCHESTER

Red & White's Duple double-deck bodied Guys were some of the first buses to have the flush glazing. Below right is L1149, new in 1949.

J S COCKSHOTT ARCHIVE

Edinburgh had a large fleet of Leyland Titan PD2s with Metro Cammell Orion bodies that had flush glazing, like that above; not everyone liked them.

GEOFFREY MORANT

On these pages are pictures of Scottish Aviation bodied Commers.
New in 1949, CMS 283 (fleet number C11) was one of six allocated to
Alexander's subsidiary, Lawson of Kirkintilloch. The Lawson fleet was merged
into the main Alexander fleet in 1961. Renumbered MC11 in 1962, the coach
was then sold in 1963 to a private owner.

The picture above was taken in 1960 at Dundas Street Bus Station alongside
Queen Street Station in Glasgow.

Alexander needed to do something about congestion at its Buchanan Street site,
so in 1944 opened this bus station in Dundas Street. Many of the buildings you
can see in this photograph were demolished long before the bus station closed in
1976, but note just how blackened they still all were in 1960.

GEOFFREY MORANT

As described on the previous page, around June/July 1949 Scottish Aviation
changed its window construction methods so that the main side windows were to
be set in rubber-mounted flush glazing, something that would become general in
bus bodies in the mid-1950s, but was very advanced in 1949. The big picture on
the opposite page is of CMS 300, that had this glazing system.

New as Alexander C28 and the last of the batch, it was sold to Highland
Omnibuses of Inverness in 1953, for whom it ran until 1961. It then had three
owners on Orkney, the second of which was Laughton of Deerness. After this,
it passed to Peace in Kirkwall in 1961, running for them for a couple of years.

It was owned by Laughton when this picture was taken of it climbing out of
Kirkwall, Orkney's main town, along Bignold Park Road in 1964. Behind it was
SX 6103, a Duple Vista Bedford OB owned by Nicolson of Kirkwall.

THE BUS ARCHIVE / ROY MARSHALL

In contrast to the multiple owners
of CMS 300 on the previous page, SJ 1315 had been
new in 1950 to Morrison of Millport on the island of Great Cumbrae,
who operated it for 16 years, after which it went for scrap. Great Cumbrae is one
of the islands in the Firth of Clyde.

This picture shows it in first class condition in Millport. This was in June 1965, and the coach was working
the service round the bay to Keppel Pier. Millport was a popular destination for day trippers by steamer and here
was a busy scene with plenty of visitors eager to look around or seek refreshments.

THE BUS ARCHIVE / ROY MARSHALL

Also new in 1950 and shown in the picture at the top of the left hand page, GSR 244 was new to Meffan of Kirriemuir
and was still with them when photographed en route to Brechin in 1964. SJ 1315 and GSR 244 had the ex-military
Commer Q4 chassis. There was very little visible difference between these and Commer's Commando.

THE BUS ARCHIVE / ROY MARSHALL

The rear end design of the Commer body, shown on the left, was conventional for the time and much the same as the
second version for the body on heavy chassis.

ALISTAIR DOUGLAS

And here is the competition: the ubiquitous normal control 29-seat Duple Vista bodied Bedford OB on the left and its replacement, the 33-seat Duple Vega bodied SB, sold at the same price, in the picture above.

Bedford's SB was introduced in the same year as the Ford ET-based coach, so the Ford really stood little chance in the market.

Compare, too, the OB's more curvaceous styling with the straight lines of the Scottish Aviation body. The Scottish Aviation style was more akin to continental and US fashion.

This OB belonged to Johnson of Scalloway in Shetland, and the SB to Ross of Balblair. The SB was at Conon Bridge and both were photographed in June 1964.

THE BUS ARCHIVE / ROY MARSHALL

The solitary example on the Ford ET6 chassis was PS 2001, shown below. Bought new by Ganson Bros of Lerwick, it remained on Shetland when it was sold to Jamieson of Cullivoe in 1964.

Withdrawn in 1978 and then stored at Jamieson's garage, it was acquired for preservation in 1982. In this lovely view in the early 1970s the coach was at the pier at Gutcher on Yell in the Shetland Isles, in use on an enthusiasts' visit.

THE BUS ARCHIVE / PETER YEOMANS

Bellhouse Hartwell also built a coach on a Ford ET6 and it too had a straight waist rail. At the time, Alec Hartwell was very influenced by American vehicle styling. The picture above shows the 30-seat prototype, new in 1950. First used as a demonstrator, it was sold to Slack at Blackpool and registered EFR 627 later that year.

A total of 14 were built. Ganson on Shetland also bought one, PS 2038, joining Scottish Aviation bodied PS 2001 (Ganson was the local Ford agent). Above right is a rear view of PS 2038.

BELLHOUSE HARTWELL ARCHIVE

the Albion Victors

All the Victor bodies were built for Albion Motors, which sold them through its dealers. The Victor chassis required a full front.

Also, the bodies all had flush, rubber-mounted glazing to the main side windows, quite advanced in 1949.

Below, BKS 288 of Kyle Brothers of Kelso was in Kelso Market Square. It ran for Kyle until about 1972.

THE BUS ARCHIVE
JOHN SMITH

The Albion Victor FT39N was a lighter-weight chassis than the Albion Valkyrie, suitable for a 31-seat body, and an arrangement was made to supply a coach body for the Victor which Albion would then market through its dealer network. 25 were built, the first five having a straight waist body similar to the heavy coaches. Although the full front made them look more up-to-date and their interiors were fitted out as coaches, externally they looked like buses. One was exported to Nairobi; Albion had a strong presence on the African continent, but no further orders materialised.

Albion made an effort to sell them in the English market, but there seems to have been adverse operator (and passenger) reaction to their unusual bus-like styling – British coach fashion was for curved window lines and bodywork. This seems to have prompted two redesigns. The first was modest and involved adding a dip to the rear windows and a curved, shaped rear end. Five were built.

Being aware of and acting upon market reaction is always important, and Scottish Aviation did exactly that. The body was promptly redesigned to the industry's current coach style, with a curved window line, curved roof and a more sloping front profile with a concealed radiator; the result had a Duple look about it. This worked, most being bought by English operators and widening Scottish Aviation's market. Five had exposed radiator cowls, then nine with the radiator concealed behind panelling, resulting in a smoother frontal appearance, plus a single example on the Victor FT3AB chassis, which required an exposed radiator cowl.

While all the bodies were strongly built, light in weight and nicely finished, the number of redesigns and the small batches produced probably meant that the work was never profitable.

Gibson of Moffat ran KSM 655 until 1966 and then sold it to a local contractor. Above, it was in Dumfries Bus Station in May 1965.

**THE BUS ARCHIVE
ROY MARSHALL**

The sole export went to the Overseas Touring Co of Nairobi in Kenya. It had a dual-entrance body and only seated 29. It's shown above left.

**PETER TULLOCH
COLLECTION**

		REG NO.	CHASSIS NO.	CHASSIS COMPLETED	COACH FIRST LICENCED	DELIVERED TO
straight waist	📷	BKS 288	72845A	Jun 1949	Dec 1949	Kyle of Kelso
		MHY 872	72846A	Jun 1949	Mar 1950	Albion demonstrator **A**
		ORB 139	72870C	Oct 1949	Jun 1950	ATO Transport of Pinxton
	📷	KSM 655	72870L	Oct 1949	May 1950	Gibson of Moffat
	📷	KBD 972●	72882L	Dec 1949	Aug 1950	Overseas Touring of Nairobi*
rear side window dip		HMJ 841	72871D	Oct 1949	Jul 1950	Cooper of Biggleswade
		KAD 951	72873D	Nov 1949	Jun 1950	Jenkins of Wootton-under-Edge
	📷	JWX 599	72873H	Nov 1949	Aug 1950	Poskitt of Whitley Bridge
		OPD 580	72873J	Nov 1949	May 1950	Plumridge of Lowfield Heath
		HSP 745	72873K	Nov 1949	May 1950	Robertson of Fruchie
curved Duple style exposed radiator		HHR 444	72872H	Feb 1950	Jul 1950	Albion demonstrator **B**
		DAG 983	72886D	Dec 1949	May 1950	Kyle of Kelso
		GET 100	72926E	May 1950	Oct 1950	Earls Court show exhibit **C**
		KDD 881	72926F	May 1950	Oct 1950	Earls Court show exhibit **D**
	📷	GET 600	73004H	Oct 1950	Jun 1951	Billies of Mexborough
curved Duple style concealed radiator		JYS 4	70791C	Jul 1950	- 1952	Albion Welfare Department **E**
		LOH 350	73005D	Oct 1950	Jun 1951	Hart of Denisthorpe
		LOH 351	73006L	Dec 1950	Jul 1951	Harrison of Broadway
		MYD 969	73007A	Oct 1950	Jul 1951	Burnell (WEMS) of Clevedon
	📷	NWE 663	73007E	Oct 1950	Aug 1951	Talbot Transport of Sheffield
	📷	FRV 592	73007F	Oct 1950	Aug 1951	Glider & Blue of Bishops Waltham
		JWF 885	73060J	Feb 1951	Aug 1951	Baldry of Newbald
	📷	LAO 160	73060K	Feb 1951	Sep 1951	Young of Aspatria
		HHR 442	73060L	Feb 1951	Sep 1951	Berridge of Warminster
		GVA 635	73061A	Feb 1951	Sep 1951	Duncan of Law

● local registration, not UK

A then to Glenside Mental Hospital in Bristol
B then to Berridge of Warminster Sep 1951
C then to Billies of Mexborough Dec 1950
D then to Jenkins of Wootton-under-Edge
E then to Smith of Inverurie 1952

* B29D body

All except the Overseas Touring vehicle were FC31F.

The Victor chassis was built with a full-front dash.

The second batch, again of five bodies, had a slight dip in the line of the two rear windows and some appropriate mouldings to the side and rear wheel arch, giving the body a more coach-like look.

JWX 599 was new to Poskitt of Whitley Bridge near Goole, and was its sole vehicle. The Poskitts ceased business at the end of 1956 and the coach then passed to Holling of Askern.

In this picture on the right it was in Marshgate Bus Station in Doncaster, probably waiting to work Holling's Saturdays-only service to Moss and Fenwick. Holling ran it until 1963 and also had a Duple-bodied Victor in the fleet.

PETER TULLOCH COLLECTION

Bannatyne of Blackwaterfoot on the island of Bute was only a small operator, but acquired six Scottish Aviation bodied coaches from others.

These were Foden CCS 61 (shown on page 36), three Victors (GVA 635, NWE 663 and LAO 160) and two Commers (CSD 178 and GUS 129). LAO 160 is shown on the next page and at the end of the book.

The picture above shows Victor NWE 663 alongside Commer CSD 178; the Commer was acquired from Weir along with the business. The Victor had five owners after Talbot Transport, passing to Bannatyne in 1965; it was scrapped in December 1972.

JOHN SINCLAIR

The photograph of the rear of NWE 663 on the left shows how well Scottish Aviation mimicked the Duple styling.

THE BUS ARCHIVE / HARRY HAY

Billie's Coaches Ltd of Mexborough in South Yorkshire bought two of the Victors, GET 100 and GET 600, and ran them both until 1963. GET 600 then passed to Walker of Slaidburn, and in 1965 to Leedham of Dunsop Bridge, along with Walker's service to Clitheroe and Whitewell.

In the picture on the right it was in Newton-in-Bowland working Walker's service on a miserable November day in 1964.

THE BUS ARCHIVE / ROY MARSHALL

LAO 160 in the big picture and to the right went from Young of Aspatria to Moxon of Oldcotes in 1963 and very soon after that to Turnbull of Lockerbie, from whom Bannatyne acquired it in 1965. It too went for scrap in December 1972.

THE BUS ARCHIVE / HARRY HAY

Sometime in 1960 a Scottish Aviation bodied Albion Victor was shipped to Gibraltar, where it was owned by Whitelock's Tours with registration number G 14149.

A careful process of elimination indicates that it was Glider & Blue's FRV 592, which the firm had sold in 1959 and is otherwise untraced. The picture of it below right was taken in November 1961.

MICHAEL DRYHURST

One body was fitted to the lighter FT3AB version of the Victor chassis. It was used by the Albion Welfare Department, and possibly also as a demonstrator, before being sold via Millburn Motors to Smith of Inverurie in 1952. It was still with Smith when the photogrph above was taken in Inverurie Square in May 1965.

The revised Scottish Aviation Victor body was more or less a design copy of the Duple, although its alloy frame was very different from Duple's composite one, as shown by HSR 121 belonging to Bean of Brechin, photographed at Forfar in June 1964 in the picture at the bottom of this page.

Others copied Duple too. The upper picture on the left, taken in Dundee in May 1965, shows a Strachan composite-frame body, HFG 605 of Williamson of Gauldry.

the continental look...

n the account of a visit to Scottish Aviation,
the Commercial Motor magazine's reporter wrote:

*"The coach body is a fine example of craftsmanship,
with vertical side pillars, exceptionally large windows
and many features of the best Continental design."*

But to most operators and passengers at the time,
the result looked bus-like and the company
redesigned its body for the third and fourth
batches of Albion Victors.

In Britain in the 1940s, '50s and '60s, there
was almost zero interest in what might be called
'European' coaches. Most British ones generally
had a curved waist rail and roof but, taking
a wider view, it could be argued Britain was
out of step.

Almost all European and, indeed, US coaches
had straight waist rails, vertical pillars and,
in Europe, large windows. Any additional
styling decoration was by curved mouldings or
paintwork, as in these examples from France at
the top of the page (photo by Michael Dryhurst),
Germany and Holland (photos from the
Wobbe Reitsma and Michael Eyre collections).

However, something similar was already in use by some British operators with what now tend to be called dual-purpose – bus style bodies fitted out inside as coaches.

With the introduction of underfloor-engined chassis at the beginning of the 1950s, there was new interest in straightwaist styling, and Leyland, Duple and Alexander all introduced straightwaist coach bodies in 1950/51.

Coach bodies from state-owned ECW, built on underfloor-engined chassis almost exclusively for state-owned British Transport Group operators, all had straight waist rails and were in truth its standard bus shell with mildy tweaked styling features, until the early 1960s anyway.

There was a general trend towards much crisper, sharper styling at the beginning of the 1960s, although a gently curving or stepped waistline was still a feature on many British coach models, with sometimes just a slight dip towards the very rear. By the mid-1960s, virtually all British coach design had moved to straight waist styles with some impressive and very un-bus-like models appearing.

Later, with the likes of Van Hool and Jonckheere from Belgium introducing higher-floor coaches with smooth, bonded glazing, Britain's remaining home-grown coach styles would develop similarly.

Opposite top left is an ECW coach bodied Bristol LS of Eastern Counties, not that dissimilar from the ECW bus version, not helped by bus-type destination screens or bus-type folding doors.

GEOFFREY MORANT

Next to it is Leyland's successful coach body from the early 1950s, designed in conjunction with Ribble. The distinctive brightwork-framed lantern windscreen was very stylish and gave this coach body important road presence.

GEOFFREY MORANT

Some of Alexander's early straightwaisted coach bodies, styled by Selby Howgate for underfloor-engined chassis, also had a stylish look, like Alexander Midland's EMS 534 in the middle picture opposite.

GEOFFREY MORANT

Duple's impressive Roadmaster on the left was probably a step too far for most British coach operators in the early 1950s, a tad too transatlantic perhaps, with its shallow, small windows.

THE BUS ARCHIVE / ROY MARSHALL

Plaxton was a British coachbuilder on a bit of a roll with the development of its Panorama model, pushing the use of ever bigger side windows.

With the increase in maximum length to 36ft for British single deckers sanctioned in 1961, the Panorama really got into its stride and the model introduced in 1962 finally ditched any dip in the waist rail and had even larger windows.

Previously, its sales had been more prevalent in the northern half of England, but with this model it was increasingly being seen all over the land. Southdown, based in Brighton in Sussex, took its first in 1963, like 49-seat 1179 in the picture above entering London's Victoria Coach Station.

GEOFFREY MORANT

the double deckers

Buying an alloy-framed body in 1948 was a risk. Operators tended to be cautious and, although the double-deck body was half a ton lighter than a steel-frame one, with consequent reduction in fuel consumption, alloy framing was new and, to many, unproven (in spite of any experience any of the managers may have had with wartime aircraft). Perhaps more relevant was the question of repair. Operators and their contractors knew how to repair accident damage in a composite or steel-framed body, but an alloy frame needed specialist skills, especially if welding was involved. It would be another 25-30 years before alloy framing became the norm for bus bodies. In 1948 it needed a large, innovative operator to try some.

Glasgow did just that, placing an order for five on Daimler CVD6 chassis in March 1948. The balance of the order was for 40 Daimler CVD6 with Alexander steel-framed bodies, the corporation describing the Scottish Aviation ones as *"experimental"*, nicely capturing the bus industry's view. It was a brave move, for although all the drawings were complete, all that existed of the double decker was an aircraft-style wooden mock up. A further order for five more on Albion Venturer chassis followed a few months later, but it was 1950 before both makes of chassis became available for bodying.

Built on a Foden chassis, the prototype was completed in December 1948. The 4-bay body had some unusual design features, some of which were similar to the Manchester ones of the Scottish Commercial body: the dip to the front upper deck windows, the vestige of a streamline swage line in the front upper deck side panel and the curved lower deck rear window. Overall it was a thoroughly up-to-date design. Operated as a demonstrator, running on trade plates when necessary, it carried dummy registration CSD 96 in a publicity photograph.

In 1949 Glasgow decided to rebody 45 pre-war AEC Regents. Scottish Aviation's tender for all 45 was the lowest and Glasgow Corporation's general manager recommended that it be accepted, though after some discussion he changed it to 20 Scottish Aviation and 25 Alexander. The transport committee, however, wanted more of the work placed locally and the eventual order was for 10 Scottish Aviation with alloy frames and 35 steel-framed: 15 from Alexander, 10 Scottish Commercial (using Crossley frames) and 10 Croft. Croft had not built a steel-framed body and simply bought in frames from Birmingham-based Metal Sections. The saga of the Scottish Commercial bodies has been described earlier in this book.

With the company's withdrawal from bus and coach work, the demonstrator was sold in April 1951 to Millburn Motors. Registered JGD 675, it was bought by the Foy family of Glasgow, soon passing to their newly-formed Garelochhead Coach Services, with which it ran until 1968, after which it passed into private preservation for a short time before being scrapped.

JGD 675 was bought by the Foy family, which had just acquired the businesses of De Duca of Glasgow and H Brown of Garelochhead, both (by pure coincidence) having Scottish Commercial bodied vehicles in their fleets.

Brown's two Scottish Commercial bodied Crossley DD42s had been disposed of and the Foden and De Duca's three Dennis Lancets, including the Scottish Commercial bodied one, were moved to the Foy's new firm Garelochhead Coach Services Ltd.

The Foden probably never ran for the De Duca business. The Foys had it fitted with platform doors some time later.

In the picture below it was at Garelochhead in June 1958.

J S COCKSHOTT ARCHIVE

JGD 675 ran for Garelochhead until late 1968. In October of that year, it was bought for preservation and appeared the following year on the Trans Pennine and other rallies.

In the photograph above it was arriving in Harrogate, turning from Parliament Street into King Street, passing the famous and very high class Louis Copé ladies' outfitters.

The Foden was sold for scrap early in 1970; a pity, for it was surely a more worthy candidate for preservation than many that survived.

PETER TULLOCH

	REG NO.	CHASSIS	CHASSIS NO.	DELIVERED	DELIVERED TO
📷	JGD 675	Foden PVD6	27310	see note	prototype
	EGA 96	Albion CX37S	60102J	Jan 1950	Glasgow B109
	EGA 97	Albion CX37S	60102L	Jan 1950	Glasgow B110
	EGA 98	Albion CX37S	60103J	Jan 1950	Glasgow B111
📷	EGA 99	Albion CX37S	60104A	Jan 1950	Glasgow B112
	EGA 100	Albion CX37S	60105H	Jan 1950	Glasgow B113
	FYS 489	Daimler CVD6	17031	Jul 1950	Glasgow D61
	FYS 490	Daimler CVD6	17032	Jun 1950	Glasgow D62
📷	FYS 491	Daimler CVD6	17033	Jun 1950	Glasgow D63
	FYS 492	Daimler CVD6	17034	Jul 1950	Glasgow D64
	FYS 493	Daimler CVD6	17035	Jul 1950	Glasgow D65
	BUS 167	AEC Regent	6616188	Sep 1950	Glasgow AR283
	BUS 168	AEC Regent	6616196	Dec 1950	Glasgow AR276
	BUS 169	AEC Regent	6616202	Dec 1950	Glasgow AR277
	BUS 170	AEC Regent	6616203	Sep 1950	Glasgow AR284
	BUS 171	AEC Regent	6616199	Sep 1950	Glasgow AR278
	BUS 173	AEC Regent	6616206	Dec 1950	Glasgow AR279
	BUS 174	AEC Regent	6616208	Sep 1950	Glasgow AR280
📷	BUS 175	AEC Regent	6616220	Nov 1950	Glasgow AR281
	BUS 178	AEC Regent	6616192	Nov 1950	Glasgow AR282
	BUS 180	AEC Regent	6616224	Dec 1950	Glasgow AR285

chassis delivered Dec 1947, body completed Dec 1948 and ran as unregistered demonstrator

sold in May 1951 to Foy of Glasgow

No 'Manchester' design items featured in the Glasgow bodies, which looked a thoroughly professional job, the rebodied Regents having flush rubber mounted glazing to the main side windows.

The picture below shows Albion Venturer B112. Glasgow withdrew all its Venturers between 1961 and 1963, irrespective of body maker. B112 went in 1961 and then served until the end of 1962 as a driver trainer, as in this picture, before being sold for scrap.

IAIN MACGREGOR

Chassis age caused the rebodied Regents to be withdrawn between 1957 and 1960. Most, including AR281 shown top right in service in June 1958, then became snowploughs or training vehicles and then went for scrap. AR276, however, was bought in 1957 by Reliance of Newbury, which ran it for five years.

JOHN COCKSHOTT ARCHIVE

Daimlers D61-D65 ran a full life. D63, in the lower picture on the right, was repainted in the yellow and green livery, and withdrawn and scrapped in 1965.

CAMPBELL SAYERS

something different the KP71

n 1949 Scottish Aviation was offering to work with Glasgow on a body for large capacity underfloor-engined single deckers. The market was competitive and, good as its bodies were, Scottish Aviation's venture into the bus and coach world was losing money. The post-war boom for new buses and coaching was waning, with what demand there was quickly moving to underfloor-engined chassis for single deckers. By contrast, work in the aircraft industry was beginning to pick up again.

A new general manager, T D M Robinson from Hawker Aircraft Ltd, was appointed to stem the losses and almost his first action was to put an end to the bus and coach work. The final two bodies were for the two experimental Albion KP71NW underfloor-engined chassis, notable for Albion's experimental 9.76-litre 8-cylinder opposed-piston engine. They were built in 1950 but did not enter service until 1952, having been used by Albion for testing and development work in the interim. Leyland Motors acquired Albion on 1 August 1951 and the KP71 project was not taken further.

The coach shown on the left at the top had a centre-entrance body of rather plain for the time, almost utilitarian, external appearance, but was nicely fitted out with 30 reclining seats. Some simple but imaginative paintwork might have transformed its looks.

It went to Western SMT in July 1952 as BSD 470 (fleet number 918) and was first used on the London service, where its performance was said to be very good - too fast, if anything. It was then relegated to touring work until 1955 when it was returned to Albion, which used it for staff transport.

Sold to dealer Millburn Motors in 1967, it became a mobile living caravan for a time before being bought for preservation, but it was never restored.

THE BUS ARCHIVE

The other KP71 was operated by Glasgow Corporation (fleet number BS1, registered FYS 495) on an extended trial basis from March 1952 until 1959, when it was returned to Albion.

Its dual-door body seated 39 and proved very durable. Here it is in the lower picture on the left.

THE BUS ARCHIVE

The bus, less engine and gearbox, was acquired in 1962 by Blair & Palmer of Carlisle, which scrapped the chassis, rebuilt the body to B43F and mounted it onto a chassis built from Commer spares.

Above is the Glasgow body after Blair & Palmer acquired it and fitted it to the Commer chassis. The added trim livened up the vehicle's appearance.

JOHN COCKSHOTT ARCHIVE

back to aircraft

Scottish Aviation continued with airliner conversion and modifications and, as the aviation market recovered, went on to build 854 aircraft. The first was the Pioneer, a single-engined light aircraft with short (as short as 225 feet) runway take-off and landing for military work. Military orders were few, but it sold in the civil market and 58 were produced. A twin-engined version, the Pioneer Two, was then developed, first flying in 1950. It saw wide use with the RAF (40 aircraft) and other air forces and some civil use. 87 were built, the last in 1970.

Further cyclical rise and fall in aircraft work in 1958 again led to cutbacks, with 800 of the workforce having to be laid off, and diversification back into road vehicles (but not buses) in the 1960s. This included building travelling shops and semi-trailers and, by 1969, over 450 commercial vehicle bodies are quoted as having been built. A short-lived venture was the development of the curious Scamp two-seater electric powered car. Only 12 were built between 1965 and 1968 and it was more of an exercise project by the design team, rather than a serious attempt to make an electric car. Several examples are preserved.

When Beagle Aircraft went bankrupt in 1969, Scottish Aviation took over the Bulldog project. This was a training aircraft and highly successful. It sold to the RAF (130), Swedish Air Force (78), Malaysia, Kenya, Ghana, Jordan, Lebanon, Venezuela and Hong Kong; 323 were produced from 1971 into the 1980s. The Bulldog was followed by the Jetstream 18-seater small civil airliner. Designed by Handley Page, Scottish Aviation again took over the project when Handley Page failed in 1970.

With a healthy order book, Scottish Aviation Ltd became part of British Aerospace, later BAe Systems, in 1978 and the Bulldog and Jetstream projects continued and grew under BAe. The Jetstream 31, larger 41 and 200 models were developed and sold well, production continuing into the 1990s. 386 Jetstreams were built and in July 2019, 70 Jetstream 31s were still in airline service: 49 in the Americas, 15 in Europe, 5 in Asia Pacific and 1 in Africa.

In 2003 BAe sold the Scottish Aviation aircraft sub-assembly and component-making business to US-based Spirit Aerosystems Inc of Wichita, Kansas, which renamed the business Spirit Aerosystems (Europe) Ltd. Still based at Prestwick Airport in 2022, it makes sub-structures for Boeing and Airbus.

BAe retained and continued the support and maintenance of regional aircraft business, naming it BAe Regional. It, too, is still based at Prestwick in 2022.

Separately, Prestwick Airport continued to develop. An air traffic control centre opened as a military base in 1947, evolving and growing to control civil aircraft. A new facility was opened in 2010 as the National Air Traffic Control Centre for the north of the UK, the south being controlled from the similar new centre at Swanwick. The actual airport was owned by a number of companies, not always happily, and in 2013 was acquired by the Scottish Government, mainly handling Ryanair holiday flights.

hindsight

The rise and fall of Scottish Aviation's bus building work broadly followed the timeline and profile of Scottish Commercial's modest efforts and, indeed, those of many other firms that had a try at bus and coach building. Otherwise, the two companies were at different ends of the spectrum.

Scottish Commercial was underfunded and, with Crossley gone, far too small to survive against its competitors. Scottish Aviation was almost the opposite – its ideas were too advanced for the bus industry. When its principal chassis partner, Albion, gave up building bus and coach chassis, Scottish Aviation followed suit. In many ways, it was like another aspiring coachbuilder, Bellhouse Hartwell, which had a similar, if more modest, background in the aircraft industry and also built some very high quality coach bodies.

Both Scottish Aviation and Bellhouse Hartwell soon found they had more success by going back to what they knew, the aircraft industry. It was easy to get some orders when the market demand for bus and coach bodies was very strong but, when demand returned to normal levels, it was very hard to sustain a lasting and profitable business, no matter whether a firm was well funded with a fine reputation and very good advanced technology, or was small and with little capital.

In Scottish Aviation's case, in buses and coaches the firm was also ahead of its time. Its uniqueness was pioneering alloy-framed bodies, which it did with technical success. In the mid-1950s there would be a growing demand for lightweight bus bodies and that half-ton weight saving in a double decker's body weight would have been significant. Had the Glasgow order for 45 not been disrupted by the "buy local" policy mentioned earlier, Scottish Aviation might well have secured more large orders and had an on-going business making double-deck bodies.

However, reflect for a moment how many of the major British bus and coachbuilding companies with which Scottish Aviation sought to compete in the late 1940s, have disappeared. Under its new owners, BAe and Spirit, Scottish Aviation is still in business.

Going back into aircraft and giving up buses and coaches proved a wise decision for Scottish Aviation. It was the conservative bus industry that maybe missed an opportunity for lightweight bodies – and a potentially great product. Selby Howgate's name deserves to be better known in the story of the bus industry.